English for the Natives

Discover the Grammar You Don't Know You Know

Harry Ritchie

JOHN MURRAY

First published in Great Britain in 2013 by John Murray (Publishers)
An Hachette UK Company

First published in paperback in 2014

1

A CIP catalogue record for this title is available from the British Library

Paperback ISBN 978-1-84854-839-8
Ebook ISBN 978-1-84854-838-1

Typeset in Minion Pro by Hewer Text UK Ltd, Edinburgh

Printed and bound by Clays Ltd, St Ives plc

John Murray policy is to use papers that are natural, renewable and
recyclable products and made from wood grown in sustainable forests.
The logging and manufacturing processes are expected to conform
to the environmental regulations of the country of origin.

John Murray (Publishers)
338 Euston Road
London NW1 3BH

www.johnmurray.co.uk

To Tracey

Contents

Contents

Introduction

This is a book about English grammar.

I know. I'm sorry. If there was any other way of saying it, I'd say it, believe me. All I can add is a plea not to run away. There's really nothing to be frightened of. Quite the opposite. Everything to celebrate. Trust me.

Grammar, though. It's a truly wince-making word, like 'overdraft' or 'funeral'. Grammar. A subject almost everyone knows they know pretty well nothing about and are in all probability embarrassingly bad at. 'Ashamed of your English?' asked the adverts which used to appear inexplicably on the front pages of newspapers. I say inexplicably: to pay for that kind of ad space, the booklet offering a cure to the condition obviously sold like *Fifty Shades of Grey*. I say booklet: I've got no idea what form the advertised cure took because despite its evident popularity, I've never seen a copy. Too shaming, I suppose: they must all have been hidden away in sock drawers or on the tops of wardrobes.

Grammar. Most of us know so little about it, we're not sure what it is exactly. Or at all. (Something to do with clauses? Are clauses involved? Nouns? Using 'disinterested' with the wrong meaning?) Actually, for most of us, grammar has come to mean 'stuff about our language we don't know and make mistakes at'. Occasionally, actual grammatical constructions do get involved in this vague non-subject (never use a preposition to end a sentence with; the correct way is to say 'It is I'; remember to never split your infinitives). But grammar has also been taken to involve mostly non-grammatical features of our shaming language use: spelling (I before E except after C); punctuation ('Chapter 28: The Proper Use of the Semi-colon'); pronunciation (the controversy about where to put the stress in 'controversy'); and especially the correct use of words like 'disinterested' (impartial, neutral) or 'decimate' (kill one in ten).

So, to make things clear from the start. Grammar has nothing to do with the way you say your words. That's your pronunciation and your accent. Grammar has nothing to do with the words themselves and their meanings. That's your vocabulary and that's part of your dialect. Grammar is the way a language organises the words; putting them in order, showing their roles and relationships to each other, adding information about who did what to whom and when they did it, and all sorts.

That's what grammar is. What almost everyone assumes it to be is a weird combination of finicky word usage and obscure social etiquette, like knowing how to address a viscount or where to place the sorbet spoons. The whole nebulous subject presided over by stern, scary men, who write books telling us where we always get things wrong: 'One should, of course, say "It is I, your viscountness". All other forms are grievous errors. Sorbet spoons to the immediate left of fish-knives.'

The sorbet-spoon school of traditional grammar has always been very keen to tell people just how mistaken and rubbish their language is. But with precisely zero foundation. Actually, we are not mistaken or wrong in any aspect of our language, and we are all absolute experts – no, beyond experts; we are geniuses – at English grammar. Unless you are suffering from severe neural damage or you are drunk or drugged enough to make walking in a straight line quite a task, you as a native speaker of English do not make mistakes when you speak.

That's not strictly true. Everyone's speech is full of hesitations and repetitions and shifts of direction and fumblings around for words.

(The social group most prone to such errors is the educated middle class, during linguistically ambitious constructions.) What you don't do is make mistakes of the kind that you have been told are hideous errors or ghastly vulgarisms or heinous misuses or abuses of our mother tongue.

This applies to the words you use and the way you pronounce them as well as to the way you put those words together with your grammar. It is not wrong to say 'disinterested' instead of 'uninterested' or 'hopefully' to mean 'I hope that' or 'decimate' to mean 'slaughter each and every one'. It is not wrong to drop the aitch in 'happy' or insert one in 'aitch' or to use a glottal stop in words like 'glottal'. And if you use grammatical constructions like 'I is' or 'You seen' or 'Me and him have went to them shops', then that is absolutely fine. However you speak English, whatever your nationality, skin colour, religion, regional origin, educational background, socioeconomic class or favourite pudding, your accent is not ugly or lazy, your words aren't incorrect . . . and your grammar isn't wrong.

You are probably completely unaware of it. You may well think exactly the opposite. But the truth is that you really are a linguistic genius. You speak English with startling finesse and expertise, and, as I hope this book will show, your use of our language's grammar is a thing of wonder and beauty and awe.

I'm assuming those sentences might come as a surprise, but they have been fundamental principles of modern linguistics for the past century or so. Another surprise might be that modern linguistics has been producing ever-more acute and sophisticated grammars of English in that time. Yet another might be that these are completely unlike the traditional grammar guides, which they comprehensively contradict and disprove. The grammatical rules inside this book are not brand-new discoveries. There are lots and lots of other books explaining the same rules and regulations; some of them technical and/or academic books, to be sure, but also countless manuals and guides for people learning English as a foreign language.

Unfortunately, nobody thought to tell us. Nobody thought to tell us quite a lot, actually. Not only everything about the subject itself, but also the fundamental revelations of that subject: that what we are told are mistakes aren't; that we are all experts and all equally so; that this is our language and that we all have an equal share in what is actually a collective democracy of miraculous expertise.

Unaware of the impeccably progressive truths of linguistics, and the scientific enlightenment enjoyed by those who learn English as a foreign language, the native population has continued to suffer the witchcraft and witch-hunts of medieval ignorance. Grammar has been taught, if at all, by people who could only pass on bits of inherited folklore and refer to Latin and Greek with the same clueless conviction of doctors who once applied leeches and tribal priests who danced for rain. The way it has been ludicrously mistaught, it's no wonder that grammar has been right up there with trigonometry for entertainment value, as apparently relevant as alchemy, as intriguing and gripping as a crossword dictionary.

Because it has languished in the Middle Ages, English grammar has remained a frightening place, populated by ogres and demons – participles, nominatives, gerunds, clauses . . . This book is meant to shine light on the darkness to reveal that the black forest is actually a verdant, moss-carpeted glade, where flowers bloom, birds twitter and the lavish picnic is free.

I know how silly that might sound, because I know that dark forest: I was lost in it as a child. My worst encounter with the ogres was probably my first. It was the late summer of 1969, when the two major events were Neil Armstrong having just landed on the Moon and me starting at big school, a grammar school, in fact. Grammar was one of my first English lessons with Mrs Petrie. She marched up and down the classroom, thwacking various items of school furniture with a ruler, this time while she banged on about the '-ING' part of the verb. I sat at my recently thwacked desk, vibrating with fear somewhere inside my vast, brand-new school uniform, desperately trying to figure out what on earth she could mean. Indefinite negative gerund? Infinitive nominative genitive? ... International ... noun ... group?

My first encounter with real English grammar happened many years later, in a cubicle in one of the language schools in Oxford. (Oxford is full of these because one of the unspoken rules of English-language schools is that they should try to have the word 'Oxford' in their titles.) I was studying to teach at one of those schools and the book I was studying was Thomson and Martinet's *Practical English Grammar*, one of the key texts of English as a foreign language (EFL), along with the Cambridge Proficiency course books and *Ship or Sheep*. Making my way through the long chapter on verbs that take gerunds and infinitives, it finally dawned on me that I already knew all of this; I seemed to have a complete intuitive knowledge of one of English's most arcane and forbidding structures. But then I seemed to know all the other chapters too, and all their contents. Phrasal verbs with 'make'? Yes. Third conditional? Yip. Adjectival ordering? Tick. The three main functions of the present perfect? Easy.

I already knew everything about this subject without knowing it. Then it dawned on me that, despite Mrs Petrie, despite my Eng. Lang. & Lit. degree, this was the first time I'd learned real English grammar. And it bore no relation to anything I'd been taught before.

With all my Linguistics 101 know-how and my two-week TEFL training, I now knew enough to appreciate just how little everyone else still knew, how utterly wrong were all the usual language guides and teach yourself grammar books that were apparently all that was available for the domestic, native-speakers' market. But surely, someone somewhere would stand up and declare the truth and come up with a book outlining the subject as I knew it now to be. Soon . . . Any day now . . . A properly modern English usage.

That was thirty years ago.

And still the traditional grammars and language guides continue to be churned out, full of bilge yet still meeting no challenge from academic linguists, who clearly regard the stuff in the bookshops as beneath consideration, just as astronomers don't concern themselves with horoscopes. I have come across one occasion when an eminent linguist has dealt with the old-school grammars: he judged that they were 'linguistic incompetents' in a review titled '50 Years of Stupid Grammar Advice'.[1]

Just as linguistics has ignored them, the old-school grammarians have had to proceed as though linguistics is an arcane technical subject of no relevance and of interest only to pointy-headed boffins. For the traditionalists, a thriving academic discipline and a wannabe science, with a huge and ever-growing literature devoted to the very subject they are tackling, might as well not exist.

That is why the bibliography in one of the most recent of these old-school guides, *Gwynne's Grammar*, typically relies on grammars published in the 1880s and 1890s. 'In many ways, the most deeply satisfying textbooks on all aspects of English are older ones,' the author 'explains': 'There is even something comforting about them – one knows, as one opens them, that the authors are completely on top of the subject and that there are going to be no mistakes or serious misjudgements.' In fact, he justifies his reliance on one author, whose books appeared in 1908 and 1898, simply because of those publication dates: 'Not surprisingly given that both are more than a hundred years old,

---

1 Geoffrey Pullum, '50 Years of Stupid Grammar Advice', *Chronicle of Higher Education*, 17 April 2009.

they can be recommended as free from even the most insignificant errors.' [2]

Right. Seriously – in what other subject could a book published in 2013 have a bibliography from the late-Victorian period and whose most daringly recent publication is from 1924? Phrenology, yes. A history of horse-drawn public transport, conceivably. But any other subject? It's like writing a book about physics by consulting only books written before Rutherford split the atom. Or, given that modern linguistics didn't really get going until after the 1920s, before the apple fell on Newton's head.

Ignoring linguistics, traditional grammarians have continued to treat their subject as if it were like common law, and gone by precedent. Alas, their precedents, the grammarians of the nineteenth and eighteenth centuries, looked for their own precedents in the grammar of Latin.

Now Latin was a fine language, one that had served its native-speaking Romans very well. And even after it had ceased to be a living language, after the Roman Empire collapsed and local variations began to evolve into what would become the separate languages of French, Italian, Spanish and the other Romance tongues of southern Europe, Latin had continued to operate as a lingua franca for the scholars and churchmen and diplomats of Europe for the next thousand years. But unfortunately for English's first – and subsequent – grammarians, the inconvenient fact remained that Latin's grammar was completely different from English. Latin's nouns were based on a case system, with multiple endings for different functions, whereas English's nouns hardly have any case system at all and rely on word order and prepositions to identify who is doing what to whom and how. Similarly, Latin's verbs came in about 120 different forms according to when or how

2   N. M. Gwynne, *Gwynne's Grammar* (Ebury Press, 2013), p. 170 and p. 175.

its actions were happening. English's verbs have a maximum of five different forms and rely on other, auxiliary verbs to help do the work. Nonetheless, in thrall to classical culture, those early, prescriptive grammarians persevered and tried their damnedest to make English fit to a Latin pattern.

The results were variously daft and disastrous but they have continued to provide much of the crazed folk wisdom of what's supposed to be 'correct' English. 'It is I', 'She is taller than he', not ending sentences with a preposition, the ban on double negatives; these and other entirely mistaken regulations still stipulated by grammar guides date from the completely misguided rule makers of the eighteenth century.

Because English is so different from Latin and so singularly lacks all Latin's paraphernalia of case endings and tenses, many grammarians of the olden days could only conclude that our language was either bizarrely simple or downright inexplicable. English is 'almost grammarless', opined one: 'words are formed into sentences by an almost invisible power, which is like magnetism'. In 1910 a Board of Education report concluded that 'There is no such thing as English grammar.'[3] Quite literally, clueless.

But traditionalists aren't concerned with explaining our grammar – it's the allotting of right and wrong that's the point of their works, the handing-down of rules that sort out the acceptable from the unacceptable. By asserting their even more restrictive versions of ultra-standard English and utterly condemning anything 'below' this, and by regarding non-standard variations with such contempt that they can only mention them with the smelling-salts and a large snifter nearby, old-school grammarians are putting more bricks on the wall that they think separates 'correct' English from the vulgarities of those who are not correct, nor washed.

---

3 Richard Grant White, *Words and their Uses* (1871); *The Teaching of English in Secondary Schools* (1910).

Their campaign is not about language at all. It's about class. It has to be, because standard, official English is the only dialect in the language based not on region but on socioeconomic group, being spoken by 15 per cent of the population, almost all of them belonging to the middle and above classes. So the purpose of all the old-school grammar guides and usage manuals isn't to impart linguistic knowledge but to provide a rulebook for middle- and upper-class membership, and keep out the 85 per cent who don't use the right passwords. They may know nothing about English, but grammar guardians can spot a non-standard usage immediately and at distance, and if they can get het up about someone saying 'It's me', then imagine the puceness of face and the vibration of jowl should they ever come across an 'I have went'.

But it's not just the grammar fiends who can spot an 'I have went' immediately and at distance. Every middle-class standard speaker can. Although they are probably not aware of it, every time a non-standard speaker uses a non-standard grammatical form to a standard speaker, it is noted. Sometimes fairly and neutrally, I'm sure, but it's rarely a benevolent response. Regional accents have always been accepted – perhaps only 5 per cent of the British population have the Received Pronunciation accent that goes with standard – and that's increasingly the case, with some accents, even those that used to be lampooned, warmly welcomed and admired. The occasional dialect word might lend colour and character (or, then again, not). But every time a non-standard speaker uses any non-standard grammar, no matter how fleeting or tiny or specific, standard speakers notice, and the non-standard speaker, probably quite unaware of it, is usually, to whatever extent, downgraded.

Standard's rejection of non-standard happens everywhere English is spoken, of course, but nowhere as thoroughly as in Britain, where language and class are most intimately intertwined.

Sometimes, using a non-standard form may not matter too much, eliciting an unspoken 'Ooh. A bit common' and no more. But there are times when non-standard grammar is simply not accepted; it's flatly refused, rejected outright, officially marked as wrong.

This is especially true of written English. In any form of written English in any public context, from office email to company report, any instance of non-standard English grammar is regarded as an awful mistake. The education system takes the same view, so much so that it is impossible to make any progress within that system by using non-standard grammar.

The same applies to spoken English and in any context – middle class or above – socially and in all professional life, public and private sector. Say 'I seen it' or 'them reports' in a meeting at any managerial level and you might as well pour your tea into your saucer and have a good old slurp.

Maybe it's different these days and the young people don't notice or care about non-standard demonstratives any more and you can say 'them reports' during a meeting at some new-tech start-up and nobody will mind. If so, I welcome this news with loud shouts of rejoicing and a bottle from a good year, because I don't think that things have changed on the class/grammar front since . . . well, pick a date from black-and-white. Or before black-and-white.

It's difficult not to sound stridently earnest about this so I'll leave it to a letter writer to the *Scotsman* newspaper, complaining about declining linguistic standards, to make the point: 'I remember in a job interview the candidate saying, "Oh, we done that in media studies." End of interview.'

There's no linguistic justification for this treatment of non-standard, obviously. None of this exclusion system has any linguistic basis. It's started and fuelled purely by social prejudice. But that's some powerful pure fuel, and standard English is very effective in identifying the PLUs from the NBGs.

It's not the conventional structure I know, but nevertheless this is a sermon that's going to end with the lesson, taken from the book of Judges, chapter 12, verse 6. As you will recall, this is the bit where the Gileadites have been slaying and smiting the Ephraimites and are rounding up strays for more smiting and slaying. First, the Gileadites try to identify the Ephraimites by asking them if they are Ephraimites. In the event that someone says he is not, the Gileadites have to fall back on a cunning second question: 'Say now Shibboleth: and he said Sibboleth: for he could not frame to pronounce it right. Then they took him and slew him.'

Evidently no one in the linguistics department has thought to tell anyone outside the department that non-standard grammar is one great big sibboleth. Maybe it's because grammar in linguistics can be a very abstruse topic, argued about by chin-stroking technicians in front of whiteboards full of algebra and gobbledegook and strange diagrams. How on earth could anyone hope to teach the subjacency constraint to absolute beginners who don't even know what a verb is?

But you don't need to know about the subjacency constraint – really, a full stop could come right there – to learn about the basic categories and the most important rules of our language, like what verbs are and how English's verbs work. And you don't need to know anything about anything at all to be told about our grammar's shibbolething. Plus, a knowledge of grammar can lead to other subjects far and wide. Far enough in the case of this book for it to attempt to explain the meaning of life in the Adjectives chapter.

Someone needs to tell you this stuff. Why has nobody told you any of this? Baffling. Oh, well – none of the professionals has done it so this is my layman's go at outlining in a lay way for a lay audience what our grammar really is and how it actually works.

So, with a brief, uncertain smile and an immediate lowering of the head, the head continuing to lower while the hand extends outward in a tentative beckoning towards the now parting thick velvet curtains beyond, here, at last, it is, for native speakers, the people who need it least, and most: a book about English grammar.

1 Our Language: A Backwards History

There are more than 400 million people who speak English as their first language. About the same number of people are native speakers who use English in official, public contexts while speaking another, local language to family and friends. Because this second group comes from countries like India and Nigeria, with higher population growth, they will soon outnumber the British, Americans and the others who make up the first.

Spanish is actually the fastest-growing first language and Mandarin may have its billion speakers in China, but with its 800 million native speakers spread around the world, including, crucially, the vast majority of the 320 million who live in the world's sole super-power, it is English which can claim to be the first world language.

That is why there are about a billion more people who have learned or are trying to learn English as a second, foreign language. Of course, no matter how hard they work or how super-intelligent they are, they will never speak English with anything like our unthinking command.

How did English rise to this position of global supremacy? What is it about our language that has made it the native tongue of people all over the planet in both hemispheres and countries that belong to first, second and third worlds?

There are various off-the-cuff theories to explain English's unprecedented popularity. Usually these cite the amazing nuance-filled subtlety of our language, its suppleness or flexibility, and especially its extraordinary complexity, usually assigned to have been the marvellous creation of its allegedly unique layers of vocabulary, whereby fancy Latinate words such as 'co-exist' co-exist with robust Anglo-Saxon words like 'live' and 'with'.

As it happens, English is blessed with one basic quality that makes it very well equipped to have become the first proper world language: its (relatively) simple, straightforward grammar. But the real reasons for English's current global dominance have absolutely nothing to do with any of its linguistic qualities. The explanations for why so many of us now speak English can be summed up in two phrases of three words each: the British Empire and the United States.

Things could have worked out differently. If the Spanish had had a better navy or hadn't been so preoccupied by the search for El Dorado, if Holland had had a bigger population, or if Germany or France had got their military acts together sooner or better, then maybe they would have colonised the world and people from Alaska to New Zealand would be speaking Spanish or Dutch or German or French. But it was the British navy that ruled the waves in the crucial period of the eighteenth and nineteenth centuries when European technology was overwhelmingly superior and Europeans could discover the rest of the planet and take it over for their benefit. The British Empire didn't last very long, but it lasted just long enough and at just the right time to establish English as the official language of a fifth of the world's land surface and a quarter of its population, in North America, India, Australia, vast swathes of Africa and everywhere else which was once coloured red on the map.

Thanks to its empire and to it being the first country to develop industrialisation, Britain was easily the most powerful country in the world, and the richest – until 1890, when it was overtaken by the nation which would come to dominate and define the twentieth century, the USA. Much, much sooner than anyone anticipated, the prospect of a waning USA no longer seems unimaginable but a possibly imminent reality – but not before globalisation had started and established American English as the international language of politics, business, science, technology, education and telecommunications. (So that it comes as a bit of a shock when, for instance, the ceremonies of the Olympics use French.)

Even though Britain managed to lose by far the shiniest and richest jewel in its imperial crown very early in its empire-building days, English was already established as the language of the United States by the time it declared independence in 1776 – easily the most important fact in English's history.

China now has its own imperial ambitions and a billion Mandarin-speakers, and there are all those Spanish and Portuguese speakers in expanding South America, but the undeniable reality is that because of the USA's dominance in the twentieth century, the battle to establish a global language was always going to be won by English – the secret of its success being, like that of comedy, timing.

Grammatical change is usually slow and gradual, so the USA became independent far too recently for American English to have developed its own grammar. Its own accent, yes, with influences ranging from most obviously Irish to, less obviously, the 'y'-less vowels of East Anglia (as in 'Noo York' and the catchphrase of the Norfolk poultry magnate Bernard Matthews, who used to claim his chickens were 'bootiful'). Some few, specific items of vocabulary also, but there aren't too many words like 'sidewalk' or 'pants'. And differences between the grammars of British English and American English are very few and either vague or very specific, like Americans not using the present perfect tense quite as much as the British do, and noticeably using a simple past instead with 'yet' ('Did you do it yet?').

The same applies to all the other ex-colonies where English has sometimes developed some local quirks, with perhaps a smattering of words imported from indigenous languages, and separate accents, and in the southern hemisphere the upward lilt as though statements were questions. But the grammar of English in Vancouver or Cape Town or Auckland is the same, and the same as in Cambridge, Massachusetts or Cambridge, Cambridgeshire. (There are exceptions, most obviously Jamaican English, which is almost, or just is, a creole, that is, a mix of English and other, mainly west-African languages.)

Over the past two or three centuries the grammar of English hasn't changed much from country to country or over time. There has been increasing use of the continuous tenses since the eighteenth century, and relics that could still have been heard then, like 'thee' and an '-est' ending on verbs, have all now disappeared. But by and large the English of the eighteenth century in Britain or its colonies wouldn't strike us as too strange at all.

The normally slow pace of grammatical change has become even slower in English over the past few hundred years because of the rise of literacy, which puts the brakes down hard on any sort of language change. (Even pronunciation. The Victorians were saying 'weskit' and 'huzif' but after almost everyone learned to read, the pronunciations returned to sounding like they looked.) The spread of literacy started in earnest in the eighteenth century, and was a development that would profoundly change society, but even more importantly created a new school of language guides. Books began to appear about correct pronunciation and spelling, the proper use of the right words, and the first attempts to describe correct grammar.

There were nearly three hundred grammar guides published in the late seventeenth and the eighteenth centuries,[4] all anxious to itemise what was acceptable English and what wasn't. Unfortunately for those grammarians, their readers and almost everyone since, as well as trying to impose Latin on English, they made three other key

---

4   Henry Hitchings, *The Language Wars* (John Murray, 2011), p. 81.

errors: assuming that there was such a thing as correct English; happily assuming that this was the English spoken by the elite, and that all other versions of the language were not just socially but linguistically inferior.

Only one dialect had been a serious candidate to become the standard since the mid fourteenth century. Inevitable choice it may have been, but that wasn't because London's English was linguistically better than any other dialect of the time. London English became the standard because London was where the people who had the power and the money lived, the city of the court and the government, and the city that has always been exponentially larger than anywhere else, with a minimum 10 per cent of England's population. If the royal court and the law courts and Parliament and the cash had been in Newcastle, then the Queen would be speaking Geordie; had it been in Yeovil, we'd be listening to the Cabinet's West Country burr, or to the Brummie accent of BBC newsreaders if the Midlands had been the political and economic heart of Britain.

Standard English has dominated our language so completely that it has successfully monopolised this introduction so far. Because all of the above applies only to standard English. Where standard has been gradually slowing down since the eighteenth century to have come to a near halt, all the other dialects of English have been experiencing dramatic, unprecedented upheaval. They have so little prestige that it has gone more or less unnoticed, by Linguistics as well as the world in general, but non-standard dialects of English have changed beyond recognition over the past 150 years. Linguistics has noticed this process just about enough to give it the label 'dialect levelling': the rapid disappearance of the old dialects and their replacement by new, much more muted and less distinctive ones.

This has been caused by millions of people moving from the

countryside to the towns and cities as industrialisation developed in the nineteenth century, when local quirks of speech were soon jettisoned in the search for common linguistic ground. The resultant merging has continued, to the extent now that many of the new urban working-class dialects have come to share many features. We seem to be seeing the development of a sort of standard non-standard.

Unless you have a thoroughly posh pedigree, if you were to time travel back to meet your ancestors (who, chances are, would have been lower down the social scale than you), you'd be struck not only by their rough clothing, rank body odour and appalling dentistry, but by the fact that whenever they opened their mouths to reveal those few snaggled teeth and talked, they would be more or less incomprehensible.

Just how far back you'd have to travel in the time machine to meet an incomprehensibly dialectal forebear depends on your forebears, but most people would have to set the dials no further back than the late nineteenth century. In the preface to his *English Dialect Dictionary*, published in 1898, Joseph Wright noted that he and his collaborators had done their work just in time to record ways of speech that were about to vanish. Taken, honestly, at random, here is a sequence from pages 604 and 605 of Fa to Gyzen:

> *gibbag*, noun, Scottish – 'a roll of flax prepared for spinning on the distaff'.
>
> *gibligant*, adjective, north Yorkshire – 'two women on one horse are said to ride gibligant'.
>
> *gick nor geck*, phrase, Cornwall – 'neither one thing nor the other'.
>
> *gibby*, noun, Cumberland and Devon – 'an old woman who stoops'.

gibbon, noun, north country/Yorkshire – 'A nut-hook, a stick with a curved handle'.

gibbet, noun, Essex – 'a short stick, used by boys to throw at birds and by dukes to throw at Aunt Sally'.

By now, most of this rural dialect English has indeed gone, and gone for good. With it has gone a long pedigree, because those old dialects had evolved in their particular places for a long time. For the entire time, in fact. Until the twentieth century, the old dialect maps still followed the boundaries established by the Angles, Saxons and Jutes in the fifth and sixth centuries.

Those are maps of England. Separate situations applied in Wales, where Welsh was much more widely spoken than it is today, and Scotland, where Gaelic was spoken in parts of the west and all of the north, the legacy of settlers from Ireland, and a descendant of Northumbrian Old English in Edinburgh and the Lowlands. This was Scots, always the most distinct variety of English, to the extent that some claim it is actually a separate language. Scots was spoken by all ranks of society, from the monarch, when Scotland had such a thing, down, and it had a thriving literature, as it does once more.

So is Scots a dialect or a language? For linguists, this is one of those nightmarishly awkward questions that you can't really answer by measuring anything. Fortunately, there is a non-linguistic definition available: a language has to be recognisably individual to some degree, but ultimately, geopolitics can do the deciding. To quote Max Weinreich's astute definition, 'a language is a dialect with an army and a navy'. Hence the two languages of Hindi and Urdu, which share nearly 90 per cent of their vocabularies and have nearly identical grammars but which are spoken by two different sets of people. Hence Norwegian – a previously mocked variety of Danish until Norway became independent in 1905 and had to cobble together a national language from competing dialects. (Actually, the

Norwegians came up with two Norwegians, Norwegian Bokmål and Norwegian Nynorsk.)

By this political definition, Scots was indeed a separate language, from the early fourteenth century to 1707 and the union with England, and since then it has been a dialect of English. Recently, the Scottish parliament has voted to claim Scots as a proper, fully fledged independent language, but that won't be the case unless Scotland itself becomes an independent country. Until then, Scots will continue to be the only dialect in Britain that can offer anything like the level of strangeness and incomprehensibility that German speakers experience all the time, with the huge differences among the various German 'dialects'.[5]

South of the border, the non-standard dialects developed in their own little pockets, while standard English asserted itself as the official and patently superior version. But before standard began to dominate Britain's linguistic territory in the eighteenth century, attitudes to non-standard English and to standard were more relaxed. Variant forms were accepted just as different spellings were accepted, the pressures of literacy and a growing publishing industry yet to be properly felt.

There were some grammatical differences that mark the English of the seventeenth and late sixteenth centuries – the still widespread extra pronouns 'thee' and 'thou', for example – but Shakespeare's grammar isn't much different from ours.

As we go further back, continuing this linguistic equivalent of an archaeological dig, we find all forms of English but especially standard sounding stranger and stranger, because the pronunciation of standard English's vowels changed between, say, 1350 and, say, 1500. It's known as the Great Vowel Shift, which sums it up, really, and it means that fourteenth- and fifteenth-century English

---

5   See John McWhorter, *The Power of Babel: A Natural History of Language* (Heinemann, 2002), chapter 2.

would sound downright weird to us. In David Crystal's example, the sentence 'We do say it's time to go now' – not one that comes naturally to most of us, I grant you, but full of different vowels – would have been pronounced something like 'Way doe sah it's teem to gaw noo.' [6]

Six hundred years is more than enough time for a grammar to have shifted in some important ways too, so although the basic structure of English of the early fifteenth century is familiar, many of the specific grammatical manoeuvres (like forming questions and negatives without using an auxiliary) are not, and some forms we use, such as the continuous tenses, had yet to be developed. The language of the fourteenth and fifteenth centuries differs enough to have been given its own label: Middle English. Shakespeare's early modern English doesn't require a translation but the late fourteenth-century Middle English of Chaucer does – perhaps not a full-blown translation but a lot of explanations in the margins and footnotes. Here are the famous first two lines of *The Canterbury Tales*:

> Whan that Aprill with his shoures soote
> The droghte of March hath perced to the roote

However, to appreciate the full difference between Chaucer's English and ours, it's important to remember that the spelling really meant something in those days, so that 'perced' and 'shoures' have two syllables and a 'gh' indicates a fricative like the Scottish 'ch'.

Grandiose claims for literature should be treated with extreme suspicion, but I think that *The Canterbury Tales* was a genuine influence on the language; first in Chaucer's decision to write in English rather than Latin or French, and then the dialect he wrote in – that of London and the southeast.

---

6 David Crystal, *The Stories of English* (Allen Lane, 2004), p. 252.

Although there had never been any doubt about London being the place where a future standard would emerge from, another factor in its favour was that London became the centre of the increasingly important printing industry after Caxton started his printing press in Westminster in 1476.

The London dialect spoken by Caxton and other early printers was slightly different from those around the capital, particularly the dialect of Kent, which was noticeably conservative; London developed quite quickly, under the noticeable influence of the dialect spoken by incomers, many of them wealthy, from the east Midlands. It was this dialect, of the merchants and squires and printers as well as of royalty, that would become standard English.

This would only happen after English emerged after a long period underground, coming out blinking into the light after three or more centuries of oppression and much changed by the experience. *The Canterbury Tales* appeared at a time when English had only recently begun to be rehabilitated as a language fit for proper communication between civilised adults. Latin had been the language of law and education and worship, and French that of the court and high society, ever since the Norman Conquest in 1066. More accurately, the language was Norman French, which had some differences from the Parisian dialect that became the standard in France – different initial consonants, for instance, explain why English has cats and castles and French chats and châteaux.

English began to replace French at the start of the conflict that wouldn't be over by the Christmas of 1337, the Hundred Years War. Unsurprisingly, during what was actually more than a century of fighting between England and France, French was dropped as the language of the elite, and English was boosted as the tongue of stout Anglo-Saxon yeomen. Another factor had to be the plague, which reached Britain in 1348. The Black Death killed getting on for half the population, labour became more valuable and English-speaking serfs more valued.[7]

The Middle English that emerged in the mid fourteenth century was quite unlike the Old English of 1065. Norman French had supplied English with around 10,000 new words, and even the basic grammatical structure had changed, from a Germanic one with different endings for nouns, and so on, to a simpler model. The collision with French is usually given as the reason for this but that might not have been too important. There was probably a linguistic apartheid operating, with little contact between the French of the pork-eating barons and the English of the pig-rearing, gruel-eating serfs. More plausibly, Norman French helped accelerate a grammar-simplifying process that was already well under way.

It is sometimes overlooked, but Norse was a major influence on the de-Germanising streamlining of Old English. The Danish political and linguistic influence on England reached its peak in the first half of the eleventh century, when three Danish kings were on the English throne between 1016 and 1042, but the continuing settlement of the east of Britain from Scandinavia had already had a discernible effect on the speech of those regions. From the Old Norse of the Vikings, English acquired about a thousand words, most of them near the core of the vocabulary, such as 'sky', 'get', 'give' and 'both'. The influence on the grammar was also important with Norse pressuring English to lose its fancy endings as two speech communities with a shared heritage sought common ground.

This was the time of Old English, an umbrella term for the separate dialects of four kingdoms. The political and linguistic maps still faithfully reflected the various invasions that had started five, six

---

7 Henry Hitchings gives an excellent account of this development in *Language Wars*, pp. 27–30.

centuries before when the Angles, Saxons and Jutes began to arrive in Britain from what is now northern Germany and Denmark. There was Kentish, spoken by descendants of the Jutes from northern Denmark in the southeast, Mercian in the west midlands, Northumbrian in northeast England and southeast Scotland, both descended from the dialects of the Angles, and the Saxon of Wessex, from the Saxons of northern Germany, which became the dialect favoured for literature and the nearest Old English came to finding a standard, official version.

These various Old English dialects were clearly Germanic in vocabulary and grammar, and quite unlike the languages they pushed west and north as their original importers arrived from the east. There had been some incursions before but those Angles, Saxons and Jutes began to arrive in numbers after the Romans finally gave up on their troublesome, wet and cold northern outpost early in the fifth century AD.

By that time there were as many as one and a half million people living in what is now England, Scotland and Wales. Since 43 AD, most of those people had been ruled by Latin-speaking Romans but they spoke dialects of Celtic. These were to survive in the westernmost parts of Britain, relentlessly pushed towards the Atlantic by the Ango-Saxon-speaking invasion from the North Sea. The dialects would evolve into Welsh, Cornish and Cumbric, spoken in the northwest of England and the southwest of Scotland. They were to leave almost no trace on English. Some place names, long since hopelessly corrupted, Brock the badger, and that's about it.

Further Back in the Past

They weren't to know it – in fact nobody would have guessed it for going on another two thousand years – but the Celtic Britons of the

Iron Age and the Latin-speaking Romans and the Jutes, Angles and Saxons all spoke languages that were related.

That sounds a bizarre statement to make if we compare Old English with Latin and Old Irish, the closest we'll get to an Iron Age Celtic dialect.

'The boy kissed the girl.'
Old English: 'Se cniht cossede thaet maedencild.'
Latin: 'Puer puellae osculum dat.'
Old Irish: 'Do-bert in macc póic dond ingin.'

But a common ancestry can be found. Let's start with those dialects of Old English. These dialects were closely related varieties of the west-Germanic language group whose modern-day descendants include Dutch and German. These west-Germanic languages all had a common ancestor, a language spoken by the Germanic people in the middle and north of continental Europe in the first millennium BC. That tribe split with one group heading for north Germany and another moving further north to Scandinavia where their language evolved into Norse and then into Danish, Norwegian, Swedish, Icelandic and Faroese.

But this is in turn just one branch of a much, much larger family of languages. Take, for example, some words for paternal progenitor: the Dutch for 'father' is 'vader', in German it's 'vater', and in Norwegian, Danish and Swedish it's 'far'. But our 'father' is also clearly related to Spanish and Italian 'padre', both descendants of Latin's 'pater'.

It was the great achievement of nineteenth-century linguists, especially in Germany, to trace the relationships among all these languages, to chart the sound changes and grammatical shifts that happened over time as tribes split and languages diverged. Some of the languages were extinct and had left behind little or no written record, but by examining its most immediate relatives, linguists could deduce a lot about unrecorded languages last spoken thousands of years ago. So the project continued, deducing and inferring, recreating long-gone languages of the ancient world with detail and confidence, beyond the invention of writing in the third millennium BC, deep into the Bronze Age.

The discoveries of those nineteenth-century scholars were conclusive and astonishing. Almost all the known languages of Europe were related. There were many separate branches but they all belonged to the same family tree. And it wasn't only European languages which belonged to that tree but many from outside Europe, too, most noticeably Sanskrit, the ancient language of the Hindu epics, which bore many close resemblances to ancient Greek, and other languages, living and dead, from what is now Iran, Afghanistan, northern India and Pakistan, with one branch extending as far east as the Altai mountains near the northwestern border of China.

This was a family tree that looked very like one from Darwinian biology showing the evolution of different species and their shared ancestors. And, just as evolutionary biology states that all life on earth is descended from one organism, just as a real tree has grown from one seed, so it was clear that almost all the languages spoken from Iceland to north India, with now three billion speakers, have a common ancestor.

Only a handful of European languages didn't belong to that tree. Finnish, Estonian and the Saami languages of the Lapps, plus Hungarian, which developed after a particular migration into Hungary at the end of the ninth century, all turned out to belong to a separate language family, the Uralic group, descended from a language spoken thousands of years ago by a tribe originally based somewhere near the Ural mountains. The other exception is the magnificent one of Basque, which doesn't belong to any language family, being completely unlike any other language that we know of.

But apart from those few exceptions, almost all the languages spoken today in Europe and many beyond are descended from one language, spoken by one tribe at one particular time.

So who were these linguistic conquerors of Europe and Persia and northern India? The evidence for their existence was and has continued to be almost entirely linguistic; there's nothing in the archaeological record of any ancient empire that stretched from Lisbon to Delhi. The only thing these people seemed to have left behind was their language. We don't even know what they called themselves or the language that they spoke, so both have been given a linguistic label, Proto-Indo-European.

Archaeologists may well have remained completely oblivious to the Proto-Indo-Europeans' existence, but the linguistic evidence is undeniable and extensive. Those nineteenth-century scholars were able to reconstruct much of that ancient ancestor tongue, piecing together a detailed account of its grammar and about 1,500 words of its vocabulary.

Proto-Indo-European's grammar was elaborate, even more elaborate than Latin's, with lots of endings and changes for its verbs and eight separate cases for its nouns, where Latin had six, then five. As with Latin, these noun endings meant that word order in Proto-Indo-European would not have been important. Sometimes for emphasis, maybe, but not for meaning, since the who-doing-what-to-whom was signalled by the forms of the words themselves.

From those words we can deduce a lot about the Proto-Indo-Europeans. For example, we know that they kept animals, because they had words for cow ('gwous'), ox ('uksen'), sheep ('owis'), goat ('diks'), pig ('sus' and 'porkos', a piglet) and horse ('ekwos'). We also know that they used a decimal system (although they may have counted in fours), with numbers that may sound oddly familiar: here is one to ten in Proto-Indo-European: oynos, duwo, treyes, kwet-wores, penkwe, sweks, septm, oktu, newn, dekm. They worshipped sky gods ('deiwos'), who were ruled by a Sky Father ('Dyeu-pihter') and they practised ritual sacrifices of animals, particularly cows and horses.

From the reconstruction of many of their kinship words, we know that theirs was a very patriarchal society. We also know quite a lot about how their society was organised: first by patriarch-led families, then by clans led by chiefs and, ruling those chiefs, an overall leader, 'regs', a term which clearly gave Latin its word for king, 'rex', but which in Proto-Indo-European may not have denoted a conventional monarch but some sort of high priest. It seems that priests formed one of three social classes, or at least functions, along with warriors and herder-cultivators. The priests presided over lavish funeral rites and feasts, where everyone drank mead ('medhu') and listened to the recitals of long poems praising tribal chiefs, very possibly the forerunners of the ancient traditions of epic poetry that culminated variously in Homer's *Iliad* and *Odyssey* in ancient Greece and the sacred Vedic literature of Sanskrit. Linguistic reconstruction offering information that no grave-digging archaeology could ever dream of supplying, we even know that the Proto-Indo-Europeans had two words to distinguish different sorts of farting and that when they were hunting, they probably avoided saying the taboo word for bear, 'hrtkos'.

Just how the Proto-Indo-Europeans said these reconstructed words has been the subject of energetic debate among scholars for the last 150 years or so. But although we can't be sure about the exact details, we do know that Proto-Indo-European would have sounded pretty strange to modern ears. For example, that final 'm' in 'dekm' or the first in 'kmtum' (a hundred) probably acted as a vowel. Another alien feature was their fondness for producing consonants using the larynx. These were proper throat-clearers which would have made the Scottish 'ch' in 'loch' sound mimsy and which they used in, to us, unlikely places, such as the first sound of 'hrtkos' or the first syllable of their word for father – 'pihter' (where that first vowel would have been hardly audible), with those 'h's indicating one of their laryngeal phlegm-crackers.

There have been many attempts to infer from their vocabulary who those Proto-Indo-Europeans were and where they came from, but that has proved surprisingly difficult. They definitely weren't from the tropics, since they didn't have any words for things like monkeys or pineapples or elephants. They weren't from anywhere around the Mediterranean, because they also lacked any terms for cypress or olive tree. They did have words for honeybee ('bhei'), beech ('bhago') and salmon ('loks'), which look promising as location finders (honeybees aren't found on the eastern steppes, beech trees don't grow east of the 'beechline' from Konigsberg to Odessa on the Black Sea, and salmon were found only in rivers dispersing into the Baltic). But 'bhago' could have meant other sorts of tree as well as beech, and 'loks' probably referred to salmon trout, which are found all over the place. All we can tell from their vocabulary is that they lived in a temperate zone with cold winters, near forests and rivers, and within reach of a sea or a large stretch of water.

From the various competing theories concerning whereabouts the Proto-Indo-European homeland could feasibly have been, a consensus has slowly emerged that it was probably in the area to the north of the Black Sea and the Caspian Sea in what is now southern Russia and Ukraine. A recent analysis by the American scholar David W. Anthony pins them down to just north of the Caspian Sea, southwest of Volgograd.[8] Anthony also convincingly places them in time, for the first time. Previous estimates had suggested dates ranging between 6,500 BC and 2,500 BC, but his account specifies a time of around 3,300 BC, when this area saw the rapid spread of the

---

8   David W. Anthony, *The Horse, the Wheel and Language* (Princeton University Press, 2007).

Yamnaya culture, known to archaeology mainly for its shallow burial mounds, known as kurgans.

Anthony also manages to fit the linguistic evidence with what few clues can be gleaned from archaeology to come up with a time-line of when this tribe spread out from their homeland. There seem to have been separate waves of migration. An early and unusually specific split happened between 3,700 and 3,500 BC when one group headed east, trekking over 2,000 kilometres across the steppes to the Altai mountains, where they eventually spoke the long-gone Tocharian languages.

The much greater migrations happened roughly 500 years later and to the west, into the heart of Europe. The first headed up the Danube, between about 3,100 and 3,000 BC, and was probably the source of the Italic and Celtic branches of Indo-European. A second wave, between 2,800 and 2,600 BC, could have been the origin of the northern Indo-European branches of Germanic, Slavic and Baltic. A third migration, to the south, seems to have taken place between 2,200 and 2,000 BC and to have created the Indo-Iranian branch whose present-day languages include Hindi, Urdu, Gujurati, Punjabi, Bengali and Persian.

The areas these people were migrating into were home at that time to untold hundreds of languages. (There were perhaps as many as twenty or even forty language families in Europe alone.) None of those hundreds of Bronze Age languages survived. Wherever the Proto-Indo-Europeans went, they achieved a complete linguistic takeover. Local languages may well have influenced the way that their Indo-European replacements evolved, most probably supply-ing some specific words, but what didn't happen was the development of any of the mixed, hybrid languages known as creoles. This was a comprehensive and astonishingly widespread linguistic obliteration. (In Europe, there is only one possible living survivor: Basque, which is often assumed to be descended from an ancient, neolithic

European language, but there's really no way of telling where on earth Basque comes from, and so far the still murky DNA results suggest that whoever the Basques are, they are not the descendants of aboriginal Europeans.)

How did this happen? How did the language of one tribe wipe out every other Bronze Age language in Europe, Iran, northern India, and much of Afghanistan and Pakistan?

There are two obvious answers, one nice, the other nasty. The nice explanation is that this wholesale language replacement accompanied an incredibly impressive, revolutionary new technology, namely, farming. Alas, the dates don't fit: agriculture first appeared in Europe some time between 7,000 BC and 6,500 BC and had spread westward at about a kilometre every year, reaching Britain late, around 4,500 BC at the earliest. By the time the Proto-Indo-Europeans appeared on the scene, almost all of Europe was inhabited by settled farmers who had developed their own distinctive societies and cultures, which was especially established and sophisticated in the fertile valleys of the Danube in what is now Bulgaria and Romania, the area that was immediately to the west of the Proto-Indo-Europeans' homeland and that was the first to be overwhelmed. This was the centre of 'Old Europe', which was one of the most prosperous, advanced and sophisticated cultures on the continent and probably the world in the fifth and fourth millennia BC. But that culture came to an abrupt end around 3,200 BC.

Which seems to leave the nasty answer; that this linguistic annihilation was the result of a physical one, that the Proto-Indo-Europeans wiped out the various societies of Old Europe and probably a large proportion of the farming folk who had spoken all those different and equally doomed languages. But to achieve the military takeover of just about everywhere in the world from the Hebrides to the Himalayas, wouldn't they have needed some sort of secret weapon? As it happens, the Proto-Indo-Europeans had two: the wheel (from the cities of Ur and Uruk in Mesopotamia to the south, sometime around 3,500 BC) and the horse (which was first domesticated in that area of the steppes at some point in the fifth millennium BC).

There are a few unsettling archaeological sites that point to the sort of slaughter, enslavement and general social and cultural devastation that might be expected of a massive Bronze Age invasion by horsemen and charioteers sweeping down into Europe and India from the steppes. But only a few. The Proto-Indo-Europeans certainly rode horses, which no doubt proved very useful for small-scale raids, but they weren't part of any grand military campaigns. And although those horses were also used to pull wheeled vehicles, these were not chariots but carts and wagons.

It appears that the Proto-Indo-Europeans' migrations were carried out not so much by their warriors as by their herdsmen. They were nomads whose wagons were mobile homes (hence their archaeological near-invisibility; they didn't go in for settlements) and who moved wherever their herds of domesticated livestock – horses, sheep, oxen and cows – could feed. And these herds were very large – the biggest the world had ever seen: a shepherd and a sheepdog can control 200 sheep, whereas a shepherd on horseback with a dog can control 500.

Theirs was a highly mobile form of agriculture, based on grazing and foraging animals. This was in complete contrast to the crop farming to the west, which had once prospered but which had been in decline following climate change after 4,200 BC. The colder, drier conditions of the fourth millennium BC meant that Europe's crop farmers were tied to land which struggled to feed them, and which the nomadic Proto-Indo-Europeans needed and would have been able and willing to pay to use.

One of their first migrations was up the Danube – 1,000

kilometres up the Danube to eastern Hungary, with five main destinations that must have been targeted by scouts, a method which also explains why the earlier group trekked that huge distance across the steppes to the uninhabited but fertile land in the Altai mountains on the edge of China. That movement west was not an invasion but a long migration, moving through others' territory by negotiation and trade and tribute.

Proto-Indo-European didn't need military conquest or genocide to replace all those already existing languages in Europe and northern India and beyond. Judging by more recent examples of language extinction, Proto-Indo-European needed only to be spoken by a dominant group with enough power and prestige to make local resident languages increasingly isolated and unfashionable, the speech of poverty and old, disproven ways.

Proto-Indo-Europeans were the Bronze Age equivalent of twentieth-century Americans: wealthy, well-fed, with wheels. Just as twentieth-century USA exported its values and language through its films and TV and music, as well as its wealth, so Proto-Indo-Europeans advertised their culture and their language with their lavish parties, when dozens of animals were slaughtered and roasted and the mead flowed, and when their bards declaimed their long praise-poems. And where twentieth-century USA also had its welcoming ideology of opportunity, freedom and democracy, the Proto-Indo-Europeans, though they functioned within an inherently unequal society, seem to have had ideas about host–client relationships that could have been quite inclusive, offering outsiders the chance to participate in their culture and economy. (Contrast this with the fate of Norman French, which didn't co-opt locals into the elite and didn't survive more than a few centuries as the language of that elite before indigenous English regained its status and authority.)

Like farming, a Proto-Indo-European descendant arrived late in

Britain with the Celts in the Iron Age. The Celts originally came from the middle of Europe and had migrated north, and began to cross the Channel in numbers perhaps around 1,000 BC. So they were not the original inhabitants of Britain. Nor were the people the Celts had to deal with when they arrived here Stone Age cavemen. They were farmers (agriculture first arrived in the south of England some time between 4,500 and 4,000 BC and spread steadily north). By the time the Celts arrived, there were perhaps a million people living in Britain. They left behind some of their megalithic structures such as the stone circle at Callanish on the island of Lewis and, most famously, Stonehenge, but little else.

Who were they? Were they descended from the immigrants who brought farming to Britain, or the indigenous folk who gradually converted themselves to farming from hunting and gathering? Or conquering invaders themselves? Were there a series of expulsions or exterminations? We don't know since the genetic evidence is still uncertain. And we have not a notion of any of the languages anyone in Britain spoke before the Celts because they left no discernible linguistic trace, not even the slightest hint of a river name, all obliterated by Indo-European Celtic.

The population of Britain was somewhere around the 100,000 mark when those first farmers appeared on the south coast in the fifth millennium BC. That's about as many people as now live in Woking. Even so, that was still a huge increase on the number of hunter-gatherers who were living here two thousand years before, in 6,200 BC when rising sea levels drowned the once fertile plains of Doggerland that now lie beneath the North Sea and separated what was then an entirely tree-covered island from continental Europe. Recent discoveries of possible settlements from this mesolithic period may bring a rethink, but at the moment one estimate puts it at no more than 5,000 people roaming around Britain's forests at that time.

But although we know almost nothing about them and absolutely nothing about the words those original Britons spoke as they foraged in the forests in small, isolated groups, we can confidently infer a couple of general things: their languages would have had much, much smaller vocabularies than ours, but would have had much, much more complicated grammars. Tiny, close-knit bands of people who don't have much contact with others – that's where to find grammatical architecture at its most baroque.

Even further back
If guesswork about British languages dwindles away into vague speculation after we go further back than the Romans' arrival, the confident scholarship of language reconstruction of any sort anywhere has to come to a halt in the fourth millennium BC with the Proto-Indo-Europeans. Any further back in the past and we enter the realms of speculation and thereafter of theory shading into fantasy. Any attempt to reconstruct languages from a time when the invention of writing was still far in the future comes up against the unavoidable arithmetic of language change: words have a half-life – i.e., 50 per cent chance of complete replacement – of 2,000 to 4,000 years.

Having said that, it seems likely that Proto-Indo-European was related to its near neighbour to the north, Proto-Uralic, the inferred ancestor language of the Uralic group that includes Finnish, Hungarian, Estonian and the various languages of Siberia. There were intriguing suggestions too that Proto-Indo-European and Proto-Uralic might also be related to other language families (the Dravidian group spoken in India, the groups of languages spoken in north Africa and the Middle East). Perhaps, the theory speculated, all these languages shared a common ancestor ... And thus was created the concept of Nostratic, a theory rather than a language, and one dated hazily to 8,000–13,000 BC, basically any time after the last Ice Age. Possibly originating in the area between Turkey and Egypt, perhaps by the neolithic people who first moved from hunting and gathering to farming. Or not. Language reconstructions peter out against that 4,000-year tops half-life.

Or so we have assumed. A very recent study has discovered that some of the most common words have a much longer half-life. A much, much longer half-life, of 10,000 to 20,000 years, possibly even more. Some core words are used often enough that they resist change: some pronouns, some numbers, 'this/that', 'not', and even a few nouns ('man', 'mother', 'ashes', 'bark') and other content words (the adjective 'old', the verbs 'to give' and 'to spit'). Analysing these, a team of linguists has posited a common ancestor language for Proto-Indo-European and Proto-Uralic, plus five other language families: Altaic, Chukchi-Kamenatkchan, Dravidian, Kartvelian and Inuit-Yupik. This is a Eurasiatic superfamily of languages of just about every tongue spoken from Portugal to the southern tip of India to the northern tip of Siberia and over the Bering Strait into Alaska. Bordered only by the separate Sino-Tibetan languages, this language family covers nearly the whole of the European, Russian and Asian land mass. And the indications from the core words are that they are all descended from one language spoken somewhere on that Euro-Asian land mass, maybe somewhere in the Middle East, at least fifteen thousand years ago. Perhaps the Nostratic theory is right: one language spoken by a group of hunter-gatherers may well be the shared, common ancestor of the languages now spoken in north Africa, the Middle East, Europe, India, and most of Asia.[9]

---

9 'Ultraconserved words point to deep language ancestry across Eurasia', by Mark Pagel, Quentin D. Atkinson, Andreea S. Calude and Andrew Meade, *Proceedings of the National Academy of Sciences* (6 May 2013). Interestingly, of the 1,500-odd words some Nostraticists claim to have reconstructed of their proto-proto-language, none refers to any domesticated animals.

Some linguists, mainly in Russia but also a few elsewhere, including the Nobel prize-winning physicist Murray Gell-Mann who has developed a sideline in speculating about language evolution, have tried to follow the trail back even further in the past, grouping whole language groups together and positing theoretical common ancestors, with increasingly dubious results.

Some linguists have even tried to identify the words of the first mother tongue: one proposal is that the original word for 'finger' was 'tik'.[10] But such attempts are highly controversial, and rightly so, because, however seductively appealing they are, such speculative reconstructing, pooling together inferences and trying to infer common denominators, again and again, has to be misguided.

All that we can confidently say is that human language has an ancient history. Even estimates about just how ancient that history is vary wildly. Some argue that language may date back to about 50,000 BC, to tie in with the emergence of human art in the cave paintings and figurines of the Ice Age. Others more plausibly argue for a time somewhere around 200,000 BC when *Homo sapiens* first emerged as a separate species in east Africa.

More plausibly still, I think, Terrence Deacon has argued that humans did not invent language but that it developed much earlier and that the credit for its invention should go to one of our ancestor species in Africa, such as *Homo habilis*, around 2 million years ago. They may have lacked the speech-adapted vocal tracts that humans are equipped with, but pre-human hominids were still capable of producing a few vowels and some consonants, possibly accompanied by gestures. The increasingly large prefrontal cortex of their brains does indicate that *Homo habilis* in particular experienced

---

10   This was one of the thirty-one items of a core 'Proto-World' vocabulary controversially proposed by the American linguist Joseph Greenberg. John McWhorter gives a clear and sensible discussion of the attempts to reconstruct a 'Proto-World' language in the epilogue to *The Power of Babel*, and rejects any such efforts as, alas, hopelessly impossible.

some sort of evolutionary leap forward and was capable of the kind of symbolic thinking which creates language – words and the grammar that combines them – and which separates us from every other species that has ever existed.[11]

---

11   See Terrence Deacon, *The Symbolic Species* (W. W. Norton, 1997).

2   How We Learned English

'I am leeving always in Barcelona but I leeve in Oxford seence two weeks. I enjoy to walk around the old big colleges. Yesterday I have sawn much of them.'

It's not easy getting a language right. All those words to learn, all the peculiar pronunciations to master. And, worst by far, all those grammatical rules to remember and apply, however bizarre and annoying they are, however lacking in apparent point or logic; all those pernickety regulations of the grammar, like the ones broken by our hapless EFL student, with those wrong present tenses, wrong adjectival order, missed gerund, erroneous present perfect and misapplied non-count pronoun.

So how is it that we native speakers would never, ever, ever make such mistakes? And how do we know about the varying uses of English's two present tenses when we were in all probability unaware that English has two present tenses? Why would we never apply a present perfect verb in a time-specific construction? How come we would always use the gerund after 'enjoy' even if we couldn't tell a gerund from a cheese scone?

As I hope you will discover, you already know every piece of grammar in the pages that follow. As a native speaker, you are not just highly competent at English; your expertise at our language is staggering. How did you achieve such masterful command of the language without realising it? How do we know all the things that we don't know we know?

Our secret is that we all learned English when we were very

young. Probably starting when we were about four days old and began to respond to the particular language of our mothers.

Just how children acquire language has been a hot topic in linguistics, and several other disciplines, since the mid sixties, so there have been many studies of what happens next. The very first analyses discovered that babies' language-learning developed at extraordinary pace, and with weirdly uniform progress, following a curiously reliable timetable.

We produced our first words round about the time of our first birthday. These words were most likely nouns, often names, very often 'Mama'. We added one or two new words a day to our working vocabulary until we hit a critical mass of about fifty words, some time between fifteen and eighteen months old, when there was a sudden and dramatic acceleration in our learning. Now we were acquiring eight new words a day, or one new word every ninety minutes we were awake. We would maintain this daily rate until adolescence. By the age of six, we would have had a working vocabulary of about 13,000 words.

This dictionary-compiling was impressive enough, but even more astonishing was the acquisition of grammar. These early studies found that young children seemed to display an inexplicable grammatical skill, even as babies. Another timetable emerged. At only four months babies could recognise clauses, by ten months they were aware of small grammatical function words like 'in' or 'with' as well as normal 'content' words with fixed meanings, and by twelve months they could distinguish new words by category (for example, knowing the difference between an adjective and a noun). Round about fifteen months, maybe three months after their first words, they began to put words together, just in time for the sudden vocabulary expansion. They put these words together in two-word combinations at first, with a score of about 95 per cent accuracy for word order, for example 'drink milk', 'Mummy here'.

There would be no other signs of grammar at this point, but these would soon arrive in a bewildering rush. Early accounts tried to pin down the order of constructions as they appeared: first the present continuous tense ('drinking milk', 'Mummy coming'), then the prepositions 'in' and 'on', then the first plurals, then irregular past tenses. But the development was so quick that it wasn't really possible to identify a clear sequence.[1]

Enough to conclude that at two years old, we were probably getting to grips with the more complex aspects of syntax. By two and a half we had mastered most of the inflections and core grammatical constructions of English, with a score of a minimum 92 per cent to maximum 99.9 per cent accuracy. And by three? A contented sigh and a dusting of the palms: job done. 'The three-year-old,' observed Steven Pinker, 'is a grammatical genius.'[2]

Parents may scoff at this, remembering the 'mans' and 'foots' of their toddlers' babble, but they notice and remember such mistakes because there are so conspicuously few of them. Besides, those very infrequent errors aren't at all random or daft but are almost always the result of over-zealous application of a grammatical rule – making a plural by adding an 's', for example.

It is an amazing progress, made all the more amazing by the fact that it is achieved by people who are otherwise so hopeless that they can still find staying upright a bit of a problem and have yet to attain continence. Yet by three years old, two years before we were deemed just about old enough to be challenged by the first,

---

1   Roger Brown tried the most confident item-by-item sequence of acquisition in *A First Language: The Early Stages* (Harvard University Press, 1973), but it couldn't really stand up and other researchers accepted that the process was simply too rapid and dynamic and varied to be given any item-by-item chronology.

2   This account is a compilation of various timetables. The principal sources are Steven Pinker's *The Language Instinct* (William Morrow, 1994) and Barbara C. Lust's *Child Language: Acquisition and Growth* (Cambridge University Press, 2006).

gentlest attempts at formal education, probably two years before we started to try to recite the alphabet, we had already completely mastered by far the most difficult subject we will probably ever have to tackle.

How? One possible explanation was the special kind of language some adults use to address babies. This is known as 'motherese' or, more PCly, 'caregiver speech'. It is high in pitch, repetitive, basically constructed and sometimes with an added vowel to clarify the consonant: 'Who's a lovely baby girl? Whoooose a lovely baby girlie? Who is Mummy's special, lovely baby?' Et cetera. But then it turned out that babies have no need at all for motherese: studies of some cultures, such as in Samoa and that of the black working-class of South Carolina, discovered that babies, who all learn to talk perfectly well, are more or less ignored until they're old enough to have something worthwhile to say. Caregiver speech might help babies a bit, but only a bit, and seems to offer most help to caregivers by providing them with an appealing – to some – way of communicating with the child.[3]

So even the specialised ways of speaking to babies, once thought essential to help them learn, are not needed at all. All babies require to learn a language as bewilderingly well as they do is the linguistic rubbish of the chatter going on around them: 'But, you know . . . [long pause] . . . I mean . . . is it on? I mean, is it? I don't . . . Ah, well.' And how on earth are we supposed to teach our children about the grammar of our language when, before the existence of this book, by my invented estimate, 98.7 per cent of us don't know the slightest thing about the actual workings of English grammar?

How in the name of blazes do babies learn to speak at all, far less with the absolutely staggering command that they so quickly

---

3 See Ann Peters, *The Units of Language Acquisition* (Cambridge University Press, 1983).

demonstrate? They seem to pick up their first language, or very often languages, on their own, quite independently of whatever blethers are going on around them.

Indeed, on those few occasions when a parent or indeed caregiver might remember to correct something they've said, children will completely ignore the instruction. Here are two recorded conversations professional linguist fathers have made of their attempts to teach their children grammar – to, as always, no effect. The first occurred after several weeks of trying to teach this particular construction; hence, presumably, the immediate capital letters of a caregiver at the end of his caregiving tether.

CHILD: Want other one spoon, Daddy.
FATHER: You mean, you want THE OTHER SPOON.
CHILD: Yes, I want other one spoon, please, Daddy.
FATHER: Can you say 'the other spoon'?
CHILD: Other . . . one . . . spoon.
FATHER: Say 'other'.
CHILD: Other.
FATHER: 'Spoon'.
CHILD: Spoon.
FATHER: 'Other . . . Spoon.'
CHILD: Other . . . spoon. Now give me other one spoon?

CHILD: Mommy goed to the store.
FATHER: Mommy goed to the store?
CHILD: No, Daddy, I say it that way, not you.
FATHER: Mommy wented to the store?
CHILD: NO.
FATHER: Mommy went to the store.

CHILD: That's right. Mommy wen . . . Mommy goed to the store.[4]

As countless parents have ruefully discovered for themselves, it is pointless trying to teach children how to speak. They downright refuse to be taught. They clearly have no need to be taught.

In 1965, Noam Chomsky offered his brilliant, ingenious explanation: children don't learn language so much as acquire it, and to do that they have to be equipped with prewired programs and an innate software designed to get them communicating. Chomsky christened this the Language Acquisition Device. He identified it before the development of genetics and neuroscience, so the label and the concept had to remain vague, but whatever it was, the Language Acquisition Device had to be a fundamental part of the human brain.

Their instinctive, innate knowledge of language would explain some other curious phenomena about the way children pick up their native tongues. For example, that they all seemed to achieve complete linguistic competence regardless of whether they are smart or dim, hothoused by anxious middle-class parents or ignored by drug-addled, underclass no-hopers. Another for-instance: all over the world, no matter what the language, children's acquisition seemed to develop along similar lines, at the same pace, until their uncanny abilities stop at a cut-off point, somewhere between seven years old and puberty.

Evidently, there was a genetic program that dictated the language-learning process, a program that only worked for the period when it was needed, and then switched itself off. This would explain why everyone over a certain age – twelve at the very latest – is destined to struggle, and, let's be honest, fail, at a

---

4 These examples are from Martin Braine and T. Bever, and are quoted in, respectively, Pinker, *Language Instinct*, p. 281, and Lust, *Child Language*, p. 118.

subject that otherwise laughably incompetent infants master effortlessly.

Chomsky then reasoned that if we learn language through the same innate mechanism, all human languages had to share the same basic features and indeed the same innate rules of a Universal Grammar. The evidence was everywhere: the same basic binary distinction in all languages between nouns and verbs, the same tree-structuring of sentences into clauses and phrases, the same way these phrases could be infinitely recursive, the same roles of nouns as subjects and objects, the same ways verbs behaved.

One of Chomsky's favourite lines is that a visiting Martian would listen to the Babel of the 7,000 languages spoken on earth and hear basically 7,000 dialects of the one language, because what we take to be the extraordinary diversity of our languages' structures and behaviours is in fact all variation on the same themes, all subject to the same controls and fundamental regulations. So much so that once you know the basic word order of a language then you can predict many other things about it; for example, about how it will deal with prepositions. English has a subject–verb–object word order, so prepositions will inevitably come before nouns: because Japanese has a subject–object–verb word order, a non-Japanese-speaking linguist would correctly predict that its prepositions are actually postpositions and come after the noun. Children don't learn grammar, Chomsky explained, so much as figure out the kind of language they're learning, consult their Universal Grammar checklist and adjust the settings on their innate linguistic programs according to whatever little valuable input they're receiving.

It was a brilliant and dramatic theory and one that would dominate and indeed define academic linguistics for decades. It introduced the world to Chomsky's concept of the 'deep structure' of language knowledge, which was converted to the 'surface structure' of a particular language by the innate workings of 'transformational grammar'. From now on, Chomsky declared, a major purpose of linguistics would be to try to identify those transformations at work, thus revealing the nature of the deep structure and the Universal Grammar which is encoded in our genes.

The theory made Chomsky that rare creature, an intellectual celebrity, and one of the most influential thinkers on the planet. A statistical analysis of academic writing has placed Chomsky as the eighth most cited author; and if number eight seems ho-hummish, let's bear in mind that these authors are from throughout history, that Chomsky is the only living thinker on the list, and that the names above him are those of Plato, Aristotle, Shakespeare, Marx, Lenin, Freud and the Bible.

I think that outside the intellectual world, in society generally, Chomsky's ideas about language didn't make that much of an impact, probably because they were presented in ultra-technical terms. But in the mid 1990s they began to be promoted with enormous success by Chomsky's most successful disciple, Steven Pinker, then a professor at the Brain and Cognitive Sciences department at Massachusetts Institute of Technology and now a professor of psychology at Harvard, and one of the world's most prominent and celebrated thinkers of the last twenty years. Pinker's book *The Language Instinct* was published in 1994 to immediate and loud acclaim and best-selling success. Pinker not only presented Chomsky's ideas about the Language Acquisition Device and the Universal Grammar to a new and vast public, he brought innatism up to date with some stunning support from the emerging science of genetics.

One recent piece of evidence had been provided by the KE family from Essex – who had recently been studied with great excitement – because some, not all but some, members had been found to suffer from a very odd and specific disability with language, particularly with grammar. They struggled to understand and produce the simplest constructions, such as making a noun a plural by adding an 's', coping with prepositions, choosing the right tense for a verb. Here are three sentences by afflicted KEs:

> The neighbours phone the ambulance because the man fall
> off the tree.
> The boys eat four biscuit.
> Carol is cry in the church.

This, Pinker felt, was clearly a selective, specific impairment caused by family inheritance: 'the pedigree suggests a trait controlled by a single dominant gene'.[5]

Pinker also offered the converse examples identified by medical science. First, the 'chatterbox syndrome' of some severely mentally retarded people who happily gabble away – about absolute nonsense, but with grammatical fluency. Another pertinent, well-documented condition was Williams syndrome, a rare disability which drastically impairs intelligence to a score of about 50 on IQ tests but which allows a functioning grammar and often overly florid vocabulary.

Pinker completely endorsed Chomsky's ideas. Here was clear evidence that language ability had absolutely nothing to do with general intelligence but was generated by a mechanism created by our genes. A promising candidate gene had already been identified: FOXP2, on chromosome 7. Could this be the grammar gene?

If there is a grammar gene, might there not be a language organ? As Pinker pointed out, language is a complex creation which involves various parts of the brain, but two areas certainly appeared to be key to the whole process: sections in the left hemisphere

---

5   Pinker, *Language Instinct*, p. 49.

known as Broca's area and Wernicke's area. These had been well known to neurologists for a long time. They were first identified by their eponymous discoverers, the French doctor Paul Broca and the German neurologist Carl Wernicke, in 1861 and 1874 respectively, when they saw that damage to these particular sections of the brain appeared to cause distinct problems with speech: Broca's patients could produce words but couldn't seem to organise them grammatically; Wernicke's could come up with fluent grammatical speech but their words didn't make sense and they seemed to have problems understanding words said to them. Were Broca's and Wernicke's areas the language organs? Was Broca's area where grammar was stored?

This wasn't a subject only linguists would tackle. Like a developing country with a corrupt dictatorship and a Communist insurgency during the Cold War, children's acquisition of language became an unexpected arena of major conflict, where the two superpowers of western philosophy, rationalism and empiricism, could do battle.

Empiricism, as defined by the British Enlightenment philosophers John Locke and David Hume, asserts that there are no innate ideas. We learn by association and experience, that's all; as individuals and as an intellectual culture. Theories have to be supported by evidence.

Rationalism, which has its foundation in the ideas of Descartes and indeed Plato, holds that there are some fundamental truths that can't be spotted under a microscope but which are discoverable by reason alone. One of rationalism's basic ideas is that human beings aren't just organic machines responding to experience but that we are equipped with certain essences, certain innate ideas and aptitudes that make us human.

Empiricism had long been the basis for science, which has to proceed on the principle that only evidence, observation and experiment can prove or disprove a theory. The logic and deductive reasoning of rationalism had found it increasingly difficult to assert itself as an alternative as science advanced. But children's language acquisition found rationalism triumphant – a rationalist deductive method had found melodramatic and clinching proof of a cherished rationalist idea, that experience is not everything, as empiricism assumed, because we arrive in the world with important innate abilities which are both basic and sophisticated.

Chomsky had been explicit about his allegiance to rationalism from the start; he first made his name with a rubbishing of B. F. Skinner, who had taken empiricism to an extreme and treated human behaviour as a simple, conditionable, input–output machine. Chomsky described his approach as 'essentially rationalist' and aligned himself with Descartes, the father of modern European rationalism. Another rationalist of particular importance to Chomsky was James Beattie, whom Chomsky credited as the man who first came up with the idea and term of a 'universal grammar' in 1788.

So the notion that our language-learning was guided by some innate gift and according to a universal pattern was not new, but it had been out of fashion for a long time. Now Chomsky had resuscitated that once-ailing idea and gave it vigorous new life. Inspired by Chomsky's take on language, innatists began to identify other prewired, genetically encoded qualities: there was the morality instinct, which gives us innate ideas about right and wrong; there was the arithmetic instinct, first spotted by Plato and given a twentieth-century rejig, which gave us an inborn knowledge about number. There was a religious instinct, an art instinct, an instinct to forgive. There was even a physics instinct. Plato thought we acquired our innate ideas in heaven. Descartes assumed they were supplied by God. Here was rationalism updated: innate ideas were encoded within our genes.

Towards the end of *The Language Instinct*, Pinker supplies his own fifteen-point list of human behaviours he thinks are probably innate, from mating to the biological knowledge that gives us a basic understanding of animals and plants. He also acclaims the work of Donald E. Brown, an ethnologist who, inspired by Chomsky's Universal Grammar, came up with the notion of the Universal People, and spends two pages listing all the universals of human behaviour Brown came up with. Some of these are unarguably instinctive – like crying and fear of snakes – but others were startling new additions to the innatist portfolio, such as 'exchange of labour, goods and services' and 'Poetry with repetition of linguistic elements and three-second lines separated by phrases'. Even if these aren't necessarily produced directly by instincts, they certainly revealed the general propensities of a universal human nature.[6]

Although Chomsky has liked to argue that the innatist view has been beset on all sides by orthodox arguments and hidebound views, that just wasn't so. The 'huge literature arguing against the innateness of language'[7] that Chomsky complained about just didn't exist. His innatism had long dominated linguistics and now the momentum was with fellow innatists in other subjects, ranging from moral philosophy to ethnology.

As for linguistics itself, there had never been any effective opposition to Chomsky's ideas, and by the late 1990s with Pinker's spectacular endorsement, there were very few signs of any. In Britain, there was one book, written in response to *The Language Instinct – Educating Eve*, first published in 1997 and renamed, dreadfully, *The 'Language Instinct' Debate*, after its author realised that *Educating Eve* was also the title of a porn film. The author was

---

6   Pinker, *Language Instinct*, pp. 412ff.

7   Noam Chomsky, *The Architecture of Language* (Oxford University Press, 2000), p. 50.

an obscure professor of Informatics at Sussex University called Geoffrey Sampson. Unlike *The Language Instinct*, which fizzed with wit and stunning examples, *The 'Language Instinct' Debate* was published by a small press, didn't get reviewed and was largely ignored.

However, Sampson did make some unsettling points as he took Pinker and Chomsky on. Their arguments were, he said, empty rhetoric, unsupported by any evidence or testing, and those few bits of evidence they had produced were rigged. Sampson then produced the evidence for his case: actual data, based on the British National Corpus, a computerised archive of 100 million words of English in use that had come online in 1995. Consulting this new resource, Sampson pointed out that far from suffering from Chomsky's 'poverty of stimulus', children were subjected to a huge amount of language – between 10 million and 30 million words by the time they were three years old – including instances of complicated structures that Chomsky assumed they'd never hear.

Sampson also scoffed at the idea of a Universal Grammar with universal categories and features. In one of his sallies, he dusted down his 1947 edition of *Teach Yourself Malay* to back up his claim that even the noun–verb division didn't stand up as a universal: there it was in black and white in a *Teach Yourself* manual – here was a language which didn't distinguish between words as nouns or verbs but relied solely on context.

This may seem an utterly bizarre thing for a language to do, a dismissable inexplicable one-off but other languages in southeast Asia and southern India don't mark any noun–verb difference. Neither is it exotic or alien. Our own language often dispenses with any verb–noun distinction and depends on the speaker to figure out how the word is functioning: many words like 'cut' and even abstract words like 'abstract' can be either nouns or verbs for us, with nothing to mark the difference. (Clothes and parts of the body are particularly fertile sources of these dual-function words, from 'suit' and 'tie' to 'skirt' and 'dress', from 'scalp' down through 'stomach' to 'toe'.)

Chomsky's innatist theory, Sampson concluded, 'has been a forty-year wrong turning in the progress of thinking about human nature' . . . 'there is no language instinct'. 'The idea that we are born with complex features of linguistic structure encoded in our genes is a myth. The English language and other languages are institutions like country dancing or the game of cricket.'[8]

Considering his book towards its end, Sampson pronounced himself satisfied that he had stripped the innatists of each of their arguments and revealed that, to cite one of his more daring flights of fancy, the emperor was wearing no clothes. The only problem with this contented conclusion was that nobody else seemed to have noticed that the emperor was naked.

However, evidently unknown to Sampson, another book had just appeared in the USA, which would be much less ignorable than *The 'Language Instinct' Debate*. *Rethinking Innateness* was published in 1996 by a group of American academics who were all firmly convinced that Chomsky had got it wrong.[9] Like *The 'Language Instinct' Debate*, *Rethinking Innateness* asserted a completely different view of language – as wholly learned from experience, guided by no innate software. Genes were important, they conceded, in building brains and in timing the creation of neural networks, and in providing those brains with certain general predispositions – to learn, to find patterns, to make associations and analogies – but there was no genetically programmed language module. Language was learned, just like all our skills.

---

8 *'Language Instinct' Debate* (rev edn) (Continuum, 2005), p. 1 and p. 25.

9 Jeffrey L. Elman et al., *Rethinking Innateness: A Connectionist Perspective on Development* (MIT Press, 1996).

A startling new discovery backed these 'connectionists' up. The first analyses of the human genome had revealed that we have about 20,000 protein-coding genes – about the same number as worms and fewer than some flowering plants. The innatists faced a basic problem of arithmetic – with the same number of individual, protein-coding genes as humans, the C elegans roundworm, favoured creature of biology labs the world over, has a nervous system that contains 302 neurons. Our 20,000 genes create about 100 billion neurons in the human brain, each of them linked, at a conservative estimate, to 1,000 other neurons, giving a total of 100,000,000,000,000,000 synaptic connections.

These first results seemed to show that strict genetic control was restricted to simple life forms and creatures with few and straightforward innately encoded programs to follow; to flowers, worms, spiders who can weave webs as soon as they are born. Our few 20,000 genes had to work in incredibly complex ways and combinations to create the DNA's 3 billion base pairs (compared to a mere 100 million for the roundworm) that build a human and a human brain that is the most complex creation in the known universe. However this still unknown process works, it seems clear that we are at the other end of the spectrum of genetic control from the C elegans roundworm. And it's very difficult to see how a roundworm's supply of genes could encode a Language Acquisition Device and an innate knowledge of nouns and verbs, X-bar structure and the subjacency constraint.

More bad news for Chomskyites began to come in from neuroscience. The once promising grammar-gene candidate, FOXP2, turned out to be involved in all manner of functions, including control of facial muscles, the building of the lung and the stomach and indeed general cognition as well as language.

Other new findings were revealing that the conventional Chomskyite account, which would have us retrieve our words from mental dictionaries somewhere in Wernicke's area and apply the rules that were stored somewhere in Broca's area, just didn't hold up. New scanning techniques and more careful analyses showed language lighting up circuits all over the brain. It even no longer seemed viable to confine language to the left hemisphere. Nearly a third of a group of Chinese aphasics were found to have had damage to their right hemispheres; Turkish speakers with damage to Broca's area somehow retained their grammatical inflections; a study of children with damage to Wernicke's area, who should have been expected to show delays in comprehension, found that none of them did; whereas another study discovered just such comprehension delays in infants with damaged right hemispheres.

Subsequent research has reinstated Broca's and Wernicke's areas as normally important, perhaps as central switchboards in the brain. One proposal is that they're the areas with the networks up and running that can handle the computational task of dealing with language. Then again, it's surely relevant that they are both found near an ear and the auditory neural systems, and those that control motor function and facial muscles. But whatever the reason and however they function, Broca's and Wernicke's can't be considered the language areas; language happens all over the brain. The conventional view of a word-storage facility in Wernicke's and grammar modules in Broca's is ridiculously simplistic, phrenology in a lab coat.

But what about the undoubted phenomenon of kids' language-learning? The staggering ability, the predictable, uniform and universal progress? Surely only an innate something or other could explain that?

Alas. Closer inspections of the data showed that children's language acquisition was not nearly as steady and uniform as the first accounts had maintained. The conventional timetable was far, far too simplistic. Children learned at very different rates, picked up different bits of the language at different times, and even employed two distinctly different overall approaches: a holistic one where they would make ambitious attempts to talk in phrases, plugging any gaps with nonsense filler syllables; and a more cautious analytic strategy using single words and simple combinations, like a telegram. Progress also varied a lot from language to language. English-speaking kids would pick up nouns first, but toddlers busy mastering Mandarin would have more verbs in their earliest vocabularies. And infants learning a language with lots of different endings for their nouns and verbs would be quicker to get to grips with them than children picking up English, which has very few endings, while Italian kids learned their pretty regular verb agreements sooner than children confronted with the much more complex system of Brazilian Portuguese.[10]

Finally, there were Chomsky's universal features of his Universal Grammar. How to explain them? The connectionists took the easy approach and replied that there were no universal features. Yes, they conceded, there are many, many features that many, many languages, from different places all over the world, have in common, but these are merely the results of us all having the same sort of brain. We also live in the same world so all our languages face the same tasks: how to locate objects in the world and events in time; how to combine words in a meaningful structure. It should be no surprise that so many have come up with similar solutions.

Daniel Everett later compared shared features among languages to the bow and arrow, a weapon which answered the universal problem of how to kill fast-moving protein sources – and other humans, of course – and invented many times over in various

---

10   Ewa Dabrowska, *Language, Mind and Brain* (Edinburgh University Press, 2004); Kamil Ud Deen, 'The Morphosyntax Interface', in *The Cambridge Handbook of Child Language*, ed. Edith L. Bavin (Cambridge University Press, 2009), pp. 259–80.

cultures across the planet.[11] My own pet example is the pyramids that are found in various ancient cultures as well as Egypt – not because they were built according to the instruction of a long-vanished preceding civilisation which must have spanned the globe, but because if you want to build something really high, and you don't have any idea about engineering and no access to heavy lifting equipment, pyramids are all you can build. Why offer the explanation of an elaborate innate software when there's no need for it?

In the meantime, Chomsky's own search for those universal features hadn't been going to plan. In fact, he'd had to jettison his proposed universals one by one until only one remained: recursion, the process where a pattern can contain the same pattern within itself, as in the nursery rhyme about the house that Jack built. But recently Everett has said that even poor, sole-surviving recursion doesn't stand up, citing his long years of study of the Piraha tribe in Brazil (the Piraha show recursive thinking in their story-telling but absolutely no recursive structures in their speech).[12]

But if they don't have a Language Acquisition Device, then how do children learn to speak with such astonishing ease and facility? Probably even more devastating than their dismantling of Chomsky's theories, the connectionists also produced their own, completely different explanation of the process. Their closer studies of children's acquisition revealed that it proceeded in a much more piecemeal fashion than had been first thought; their first word combinations in the second year of life weren't grammatical, as had been reported, and were evidently based not on any rule-seeking machinery but on specific structures involving particular

11   Daniel Everett, *Language: The Cultural Tool* (Profile Books, 2012).

12   Ibid.

words; these were 'island constructions' which children seemed to rely on for the first three years, with no visible symptoms of any general understanding of any grammatical regulations. Rather than spotting and applying rules, children appeared to learn conventions through fixed phrases at first before they progressed to more abstract patterns. There was no innate machine operating kids; they picked up language only from their experience: 'children can only learn what they are exposed to'.[13]

The only innatist idea that did seem to hold water was that of the critical period. Undeniably, language-learning was very easy for the very young and very difficult for everyone else. But there was a new theory to explain that as well: the less-is-more hypothesis. The very immaturity of young brains helps them learn, by allowing them to start small and grow big, knowledge developing as the brain develops.[14]

This new connectionist theory has been enthusiastically welcomed by neuroscience, which is not surprising since the theory is also designed in accordance with the latest models of how our brains work. Of course, we still know next to nothing about the neural processes in our heads, but what little we do know indicates that our brains are constructed of uncountable trillions of neural networks, with many, many, many connections to other such networks all over the brain. These are much more sophisticated than the simple input–output, stimulus–response devices of Skinner's mechanistic view, because mediating between input and output, feeding backwards and forwards between the two are 'hidden units'.[15]

13 This quote is from p. 110 of Michael Tomasello's *Constructing a Language: A Usage-Based Theory of Language Acquisition* (Harvard University Press, 2003), one of the clearest and most influential of the connectionist accounts. I have also drawn for this summary on Dabrowska's *Language, Mind and Brain*.

14 The less-is-more hypothesis was first proposed by Elissa Newport in 'Maturational Constraints in Language Learning', *Cognitive Science* 14 (1990), pp. 11–28.

15 This is outlined in, for example, Stephen E. Nadeau, *The Neural Architecture of*

For 'hidden' read 'completely unknown and guessed at'. But as yet crude computer models of such neural networks have been shown to learn grammar categories and operations – sorting out nouns from verbs, getting the past tenses right for regular and irregular verbs – on simple, distributional grounds. Most excitingly of all, these computer-model networks acquire language in a way that replicates the manner of children's learning, with the same bursts of development that are characteristic of dynamically evolving systems, and with the same U-shaped development as conventions are followed then broken by over-generalised rule applications which are then corrected.

Reflecting on the theory they were replacing, the connectionist collective of *Rethinking Innateness* marvelled at the strong appeal which innatism had clearly held. They instanced the response to the KE family. Why had the news about the 'language mutants' been so eagerly received? The news about the KEs had appeared originally only in a brief letter to *Nature*, but it had been seized on and proclaimed wide and far. Unlike the next report, which had been completely ignored; the one that established that all affected KE members suffered from general cognition problems, not just language. 'There seems to be a deep-rooted desire to believe that humans are not only unique (every species is unique after all) but that our uniqueness arises from a quantum leap in evolution. The grammar gene satisfies this desire.'[16]

Because there simply could not be one, there was no case against his theories, Chomsky asserted in 2000.[17] But by that time, the case

---

Grammar (MIT Press, 2012).

16 Elman et al., *Rethinking Innateness*, p. 378.

17 '[P]eople who are proposing that there is something debatable about the assumption that language is innate are just confused. So deeply confused that there is no way of answering their arguments' (*Architecture of Language*, p. 51).

against Chomsky had already been made, and it was based not only on necessarily theoretical computer modelling but on the hard facts and data of empirical research.

Linguistics was now split between the old guard, who still believed in Chomsky, and the new school of the connectionists. There have been attempts to reconcile the two camps. (Steven Pinker makes a valiant effort in *Words and Rules*,[18] proposing that the empiricists are right about some aspects of language acquisition and rationalist innatists about others.) But really, these have been doomed to failure. There isn't any room for the grey of compromise because it's a black and white issue. Either we are all born with the innate software of a Language Acquisition Device and a Universal Grammar or we are not.

And it very much seems that we are not.

There are two reasons to back the connectionists. One is that their case is very strong; it's straightforward and coherent, it's backed up by evidence, and it hasn't met any stumbling blocks so far. The second is that Chomsky's theories exhibit all the main symptoms of error: they have not been supported by any evidence but only by other theories, all of them dubious at best or simply disproved; they are ultra-complicated, and instead of providing answers only beg more questions. (What precisely is this Language Acquisition Device? Where is it? How do our genes build it?)

Since all Chomsky's work was based on his innatist idea, and all his theories were created to try to explain it in operation, I struggle to see what, if anything, can survive of it if he is as wrong as he seems to be. The theta transformation, the subjacency constraint, the pro-drop parameter, and all the other parameters and principles and transformations; if there is no Universal Grammar or deep structure, then I can't see how any product of his theoretical work can avoid

---

18 Steven Pinker, *Words and Rules: The Ingredients of Language* (Basic Books, 1999).

going the way of the Language Acquisition Device, into the dustbin of discredited notions, on top of the four humours of the body, phlogiston and indeed phrenology.

It seems to me that all that's left are the very serious questions that have to be asked of the academic discipline he has dominated for four or five decades. How were his theories accepted so readily? Why were they never tested? Or even questioned?

Part of the reason has to be that Chomsky's ingenuity and intelligence are such that the theories he created are intimidatingly brainy. They are also outlined in a jargon that he created and his even more forbidding algebra. As a result, his transformational grammar was acclaimed by disciples and avoided as much as possible by everyone else. Just as intimidating is Chomsky himself, for he is a formidable figure. Who would risk an academic career to tangle with a genius over Linguistics' equivalent of string theory?

Nobody, as it turned out, for more than thirty years.

If Chomsky is as wrong as he seems to be, the consequences for Linguistics are profound and fairly disastrous. Because if he is wrong, then Linguistics, which aspires to be a science, has allowed its theoretical branch to have become a twentieth-century alchemy. And by unquestioningly accepting Chomsky's assumptions, Linguistics has managed to neglect some fundamental and important issues.

For basic example: is there a link between grammar usage and general intelligence? Or reading ability? Or educational level? There is hardly any research on any of these topics, these being issues Chomskyites wouldn't even consider, what with us all having the same magical equipment that gave us all the same complete theoretical knowledge.

What about class? Might the socioeconomic background affect grammar use? Sorry, nothing really on that either. There is one much-cited because so rare study of language acquisition by class, by two American researchers. What they studied wasn't grammar use but the linguistic experience of the child. It's not much but it's about all that Linguistics has so far come up with by way of research on this issue, and even those findings were very disturbing.

It seems that the more a child is talked to and responded to, and the more encouraging and positive that response, the greater and faster the development in language and IQ score. (It has to be face-to-face interaction; watching CBeebies doesn't help.) Very depressingly, this equates strongly to socioeconomic status, i.e., class. Children whose parents were on welfare heard an average of 600 words an hour addressed to them, children with parents in blue-collar jobs 1,200, and children of professionals 2,100. The discrepancies become more marked as the years go by.

Income	After one week	After one year	After four years
High	215,000	11 million	44 million
Middle/lower	125,000	6 million	24 million
On welfare	62,000	3 million	12 million[19]

Moreover, the higher up the social ladder, the more positive the parental contribution tends to be, while the lower down that ladder, the more frequent the stop-thats and shut-ups: in the group on welfare, 20 per cent of parents' utterances to kids were to forbid, whereas nearly 50 per cent of the middle-income group's interactions were questions. Does this matter, or do we all attain the same super-competence anyway? Or are we all linguistic geniuses but with differing degrees of geniusness?

---

19 B. Hart and T. R. Risley, 'American Parenting of Language-learning Children', *Developmental Psychology* 28 (1992), pp. 1096–1105, quoted in Eve V. Clark, *First Language Acquisition* (Cambridge University Press, 2nd edn, 2009), p. 45.

Here's another unanswered question: if it is a product of a culture, can the actual grammar of a language be affected or even determined by that culture? There seem to be some indications that it might well be, including evidence from the most ancient writings, which seem to lack complex structures that writing itself seems to have developed. Is that a matter of writing and its conventions or does it reflect some reality, i.e., did people not use subordinate clauses before writing was invented?[20]

Ultimately, all this loose talk of potential differences and discrepancies opens a door which Chomsky and many others thought they'd shut for good in the fifties, and beckons in the awkward, cringe-inducing Sapir–Whorf hypothesis. At its baldest, the Sapir–Whorf hypothesis states that the language you speak determines the way you look at the world, with each language providing its own view of the world. This would mean that there are 7,000 different lenses through which humans view the world, 7,000 different linguistically determined mindsets. Taken to an extreme, this could imply that although our language is a collective creation, we are also trapped in our own individually customised versions of it. Milder, slightly more palatable versions of the Sapir–Whorf hypothesis have also been tentatively, apologetically forwarded. But however it's applied, the Sapir–Whorf hypothesis proposes that language may fundamentally divide us. It's a really unpopular, unlikeable theory, but if there are no such things as language universals, then the Sapir–Whorf hypothesis has to be reconsidered. This process is already under way – for example, the leading neurolinguist Jerome Feldman is confident that 'the language people speak does have a measurable effect on how they think' and that

---

20 Guy Deutscher showed the progression to complexity in *Syntactic Change in Akkadian* (Oxford University Press, 2000) and, more briefly and with greater reader-friendliness, in *The Unfolding of Language* (Henry Holt, 2005), pp. 222ff.

'grammatical form clearly has some measureable effects on cognition'.[21]

With the demise of Universal Grammar, all the interesting work now being done on language is being conducted by connectionists and theoreticians whose work is firmly grounded on empiricist principles. One of the new thinkers is Daniel Everett, who has for many years been studying the life and very odd language of the Piraha tribe in the Amazonian rainforest. Everett proposes that language is a learned skill, a 'cultural tool', and that each language is the collective expression and product of a particular culture. Like others, he dismisses the idea that there could be any universal features of human language, citing not only the lack of certain supposedly key recursive structures but the lack of number in Piraha as evidence.[22]

Another impressive contribution has been made by the American evolutionary biologist-cum-neuroscientist Terrence Deacon. Unfortunately, he's not a great writer, relying on technical terminology and lots and lots of dry detail, which both do their best to hide the several fascinating ideas in his book, *The Symbolic Species*. One of those ideas offers a very astute and convincing explanation of how we can acquire language so amazingly as children: because our brains and our languages have co-evolved.

For a primate our size, our brains are three times larger than they should be. Most of the expansion is in the massively enlarged and super-active prefrontal cortex, which has an estimated squillion connections to other areas. Deacon dates the start of this cortical expansion to about 2 million years ago, when he thinks pre-human hominids could have invented the first, basic language.

---

21   Jerome A. Feldman, *From Molecule to Metaphor* (MIT Press, 2006), p. 190 and p. 193.
22   Everett, *Language: The Cultural Tool*.

However, dramatic though our brain evolution has been, Deacon reasons, most of the evolving must have been done by languages themselves, the process of linguistic evolution being a whole lot quicker and easier than biological evolution. And indeed, if you think about it, languages are always under intense evolutionary selection pressure. Their only method of survival is to be transmitted from one generation to the next. So they have to be able to be learned by the children who are going to be doing the transmitting. Their very existence is at stake. As Deacon observes, 'languages need children more than children need languages'.[23]

Oddly, it seems that what suits children most is a fiendishly complicated grammar. Lots of suffixes and prefixes and agreements for their nouns, verbs looping the loop to specify when and how and possibly by what means and even by whose evidence something may, could or definitely did happen. Lots and lots of grammatical flourishes; that's what infants like. Possibly because it helps them learn by relying less on context. And maybe lots of endings and prefixes and what-have-you provide toddlers with multiple cues and clues.[24]

Young children's desire for complexity in their grammar would explain why, when left to its own devices, spoken by a small clan of people and no interlopers, depending for its survival only on oral transmission from one generation to the next, a language will veer towards the baroque and acquire all manner of ornaments and folde-rols. By the same token, the more popular and widespread a language, the more complicated its society and culture, the simpler it will become, as it adjusts to being learned by adults as well as kids. Hence the commitment to simplicity of English.

---

23   Deacon, *Symbolic Species*, p. 109.

24   These intriguing explanations are forwarded by Gary Lupyan and Rick Dale in their paper, 'Language Structure is Partly Determined by Social Structure', available online at plosone.org

Deacon also asks one of the questions linguistics hasn't: why don't any other animals have language? Some of those animals are very clever, many have communication systems, and the evolutionary advantages of even a basic sort of language are many and various. Yet no other species has ever had anything remotely like a language, not even the simplest kind, with one or two dozen words and just one or two grammatical rules. Some animals will respond to specific calls, and dogs seem to grasp the meaning associations of a small vocabulary, but no animals seem to *get* language in the sense of acquiring it or of understanding its basic nature.

What seems to be beyond other animals' comprehension, says Deacon, is language's basis as a symbolic system. Other animals have communication systems but they are all based on one-to-one correspondences. Michael Tomasello takes the instructive example of the vervet monkey, which has different alarm calls for snakes, eagles and leopards.[25] These aren't separate words but simply one-to-one calls: see snake, make snake-alert noise. These calls are innate, instinctive, and work as you'd expect an instinct to: vervet monkeys raised in isolation will still produce those calls, vervet monkeys cannot be taught new ones, and can't produce a call without the emotional trigger of the fear created by the predator; they continue to make their alarm calls even after every other monkey has been successfully alerted, even after the predator has gone and will make those calls as long as they're still frightened.

Of course, unlike vervet monkeys, some species can learn a new communication system, as every dog owner knows, but what they learn are more one-to-one associations: food, walk in park, come here. Only humans look at individual examples of something and try to make abstract patterns and categories from them. Only humans

---

25   Michael Tomasello, *Origins of Human Communication* (MIT Press, 2008), pp. 15–16.

can use words – sounds which are symbols – because they don't name individual things but the categories, the ideas of the things. Grammar, the rules, conventions and principles which govern these symbols in operation, is itself a symbolic system of symbols organising symbols of symbols, like a ten-pound note is the symbol of a symbol (money) which is in turn the notional symbol (economic value) of a symbol (the abstract worth of a provision or service). You may as well ask a vervet monkey to open a bank account as expect it to talk.

To develop a language, you need to think symbolically. Animals can't. Nor can they make another mental leap that Michael Tomasello has spotted as being crucial to the whole human enterprise of 'co-operative communication': theory of mind, the realisation that other people exist as fully as yourself. To make any effort at communication with someone else, you first have to realise that there is someone else with a mind like but separate from yours to communicate with. The sharing of attention and intention is something that comes naturally to humans but no other species. To take the most basic example, pointing seems to be a genuine universal human trait; by fourteen months old a human baby from any culture will be able to interpret a pointing gesture and look in the appropriate direction. But other primates just don't get this at any age. The absence of any co-operative basis for their communication systems explains the behaviour of macaque monkey mothers who, seeing a predator threaten their offspring, but safe themselves, will not give an alarm call.[26]

Only humans have the theory of mind that makes language possible. Only humans have the enormous brain capacity needed for the symbolic thinking needed to create words and organise them with grammar. Two very convincing reasons to explain why, despite

---

26 Ibid., p. 18.

countless efforts with whole zoos of chimps and dolphins and talking parrots, no other animal has ever shown the teensiest sign of language.

With one exception: Kanzi.

Now an elderly thirty-three, Kanzi is a bonobo chimpanzee who lives at the Great Ape Trust in Des Moines in Iowa. He is quite unlike all the other chimps who have been taught to use forms of language using hand-signing or keyboard word-signs called 'lexigrams'. After long and persistent coaching, chimps can understand some signs and produce a series of repetitive statements, usually demands for food, with no use of the signs as symbols; these remain one-to-one associations. Nor is there any evidence at all of any organising grammar. Here is the translation from American Sign Language of a chimp asking for a banana: 'You me banana me banana you.' This is how a chimp asked for an orange: 'Give orange me give eat orange me eat orange give me eat orange give me you.'[27]

Kanzi is different. It's not the size of his relatively extensive vocabulary that's impressive – he understands thousands of words and can use nearly five hundred – so much as the way he seems to be able to deal with individual lexigrams, evidently treating them as symbols and, remarkably, following his own basic but consistent word order in producing them. And, unlike all the other chimps, Kanzi seems able to understand the grammar of spoken English. Given an instruction, even some bizarre one he wouldn't have come across before, Kanzi will show an understanding not only of its words but of its grammatical structure. So, when he was told, 'Put the keys in the refrigerator', Kanzi evidently figured out the word order and took note of the preposition 'in', and he placed the keys inside the fridge.

---

27   Quoted by Pinker in *The Language Instinct*, pp. 339 and 340.

The evolution will be televised: there are some amazing videos on YouTube that show Kanzi dutifully putting the keys in the fridge . . . and making and using tools . . . and making a fire . . . then spearing a marshmallow on a stick and toasting it. According to his Wikipedia entry, when Kanzi was in a group of bonobos who were presented with a Maori 'haka' war dance, his reaction was unique. All the other bonobos responded to the haka's display of aggression by slapping the floor and shrieking and baring their teeth; Kanzi was calm and intrigued and asked to see the dance again, away from all the racket, in a private performance so that the other bonobos wouldn't get upset. The nature of his vocal tract means that Kanzi can't speak, but he does seem to produce particular sounds that accompany the symbols of the two systems he has acquired, keyboard lexigrams and American Sign Language.

Strangely but very significantly, and cocking a final snook at the innatists' assumption that only some magic could explain the miracle of children's language acquisition, Kanzi wasn't taught either system. The researchers were actually teaching his adopted mother, Matata, while Kanzi clung on to her and generally got in the way of the experiment. Matata turned out to be every bit as poor a language-learner as all the other chimps who'd been given systematic and careful instruction. However, when the researchers thought Kanzi was just about old enough to start learning sign language, they discovered that he already knew most of it. He had already acquired the rules of this communication game for himself, as a baby.

How? As many a chimpanzee language coach had found out the hard way, baby chimps are far too distractable to be taught anything at all, and are just not up to any arduous task. But Kanzi wasn't taught. He didn't need to be taught: mere exposure helped him create a language module for himself. And he managed it because he was very, very young. Newborn chimps are more mature than human babies, arriving in the world at a developmental stage humans take a good year to reach, so it seems that the time for a chimp to learn a language as we do is soon after birth. Language can only be picked up by immature brains – bit by bit, developing as the baby's brain develops. Kanzi is convincing proof of the less-is-more hypothesis.

We have no idea how he did it, but Kanzi also crossed the 'symbolic threshold'; he understood the abstract nature of words. He'd got language because he'd got what it was and how it worked.[28]

So that's another boundary fuzzed. Or rubbed out. Just when we had discovered symbolic language as a feature that definitely separates us from the rest of the animal kingdom, drawing a sharp line between us and below us, providing a unique and essential and defining attribute of the unparalleled magnificence of humans, along comes Kanzi, putting the keys in the fridge.

Kanzi is living, clinching proof that language is not produced by some innate programming magic that only us humans possess. A language instinct? How could there be such a thing? We are the least instinctive species on earth, arriving here equipped with the abilities to suckle and produce a distress call and . . . that's about it. Language is the diametric opposite of an instinct. It's entirely learned, entirely from experience.

As for language itself, that is a collective, cultural construction. All of us and each of us is part of it. English really is our language.

We all started to learn our English young – four days after birth if our mothers spoke English – and our knowledge of English grew as

---

28   The phrase is gratefully appropriated from Terrence Deacon. Kanzi's principal tutor, Sue Savage-Rumbaugh, and Roger Lewin describe his extraordinary achievements in *Kanzi: The Ape at the Brink of the Human Mind* (Wiley, 1994).

our neural networks grew. Until our brains were fizzing with trillions of neural networks of trillions and trillions of intricately connected neurons and we had grown into the full present-perfect-passive mastery we all now possess.

Despite the fact that we don't have a blessed clue how any of it actually works.

3   Nouns

All human languages are based on two sorts of word: nouns, the words for things; and verbs, the words for actions. 'The boy [noun] kicked [verb] the ball [noun].' 'Aardvark', 'biscuit', 'conman', 'dishwasher', 'Ebeneezer' . . . 'xylophone', 'yurt' and 'Zanzibar', and all the other words and names for things, people and places, they're all nouns.

Well, usually, mostly and sort of. As in life, language is more complicated than hard-and-fast definitions allow, so we'll return to the instructively challenging business of defining what exactly a noun is at the end of this chapter. In the meantime, let's accept the traditional, thingy-based explanation and move on to acknowledge that at least half of your vocabulary consists of nouns, which, at a rough estimate, outnumber your verbs by three to one.

How many words do you think you know? Estimates of just how large someone's vocabulary might be vary wildly, not reflecting any prejudgement about their age, intelligence or education but the sheer difficulty of the task, starting with the basic problem of defining the term 'word'. Do different forms of the same word count as separate? Or different meanings? Or functions? Take 'well': that turns up as an adjective, an adverb, a noun, a verb and an exclamation, and has dozens of separate meanings. So guesses range between an average passive vocabulary (i.e., of words recognised if not used) of about 40,000 for a university student to over 70,000 words for a university lecturer (though that guess was made by a university lecturer).[1]

---

1   David Crystal, *The Cambridge Encyclopedia of the English Language* (Cambridge University Press, 1995), p. 123.

Managing the evidently controversial task of leaving their university department, two American linguists came up with an estimate of about 60,000 words for someone with a high-school education.[2] The 20-volume *Oxford English Dictionary* contains about a quarter of a million words, but that doesn't include technical terms, words that have been too recently coined to gain admission or dialect words. Including all those gives English a rough-and-ready word total of three-quarters of a million.

It's impossible to say for certain, but English probably boasts the largest vocabulary of any language ever spoken. There are several reasons for this. One is the historic accident which meant that English acquired separate layers of vocabulary from Anglo-Saxon, Latin and French. Another reason is English's willingness to absorb words from other languages. Of those quarter of a million words in the *Oxford English Dictionary*, 99 per cent are borrowed from other languages, mainly from Latin and French but also from more than 350 others, from Afrikaans aardvark and Greenlandic Inuit anorak to ziggurat from Akkadian, a long-extinct language spoken 4,000 years ago in Mesopotamia. A third factor explaining English's vast word count is that it is written down. Oral languages – ones that are only spoken – have much, much smaller vocabularies, usually between 3,000 to 5,000 words. Because an oral language can't have a passive vocabulary – if a language doesn't have writing, words that aren't used cease to exist.

Having avoided the murky business of definition for the moment, let's skip blithely on to the forms that English's nouns take. Theoretically, these could be simpler, but not by much. For a start, English's nouns aren't divided into subcategories, unlike most other European languages, which sort their nouns into different genders; for example, French has a masculine 'cloud' ('le nuage') and feminine 'rain'

---

2   Cited by Pinker in *The Language Instinct*, p. 150.

('la pluie'), Spanish has a feminine 'cloud' ('la nube') and a masculine 'sky' ('el cielo'), and German has a masculine 'sky' ('der Himmel') and 'sunshine' ('der Sonnenschein') but a feminine 'Sun' ('die Sonne') and a neuter 'storm' ('das Unwetter').

Traditionally, at this point there would be a mention of the gender distinctions in some of English's nouns, like 'duke/duchess' or 'waiter/waitress', but those often sexist pairings[3] don't constitute different grammatical groupings because they don't affect the construction of the rest of the sentence. The noun 'actress' behaves exactly the same as 'actor' does and has no influence on, say, adjectives, as words of different genders do in French, or on the endings of verbs, as in Russian.

Besides, this is to misunderstand the meaning of gender in this context. As a grammatical term, 'gender' refers to a group or class of nouns, not their sex. As it happens, those of the world's languages which do have different genders of nouns – just under half – mostly do base their noun classes on a male–female difference, however arbitrary (why are French clouds masculine? Why is French rain female?) or even counterintuitively bizarre, as with German, which, as Mark Twain pointed out, has female turnips but neuter maidens, and all sorts.[4] But lots of languages have non-sexual categories for their subgroups of nouns, usually based on a distinction between animate and inanimate. The Australian Aboriginal language of Dyirbal, for example, now spoken by just five people in northeast Queensland, has four kinds of nouns, which are allocated to separate groups according to the following criteria: (1) male humans plus most non-human creatures; (2) female humans, water, fire, fighting and dangerous animals; (3) edible fruit and vegetables; and (4) everything else.

---

3 Condescending female variants like 'poetess' and 'authoress' are already on their way out, with moves afoot to jettison others, including 'actress' and indeed 'waitress'.

4 Mark Twain, *The Awful German Language* (1880).

Whereas most European languages are restricted to a maximum of the three, sex-based genders – male, female and neuter – which operated in Proto-Indo-European, others, particularly in the Niger-Congo family of languages in west Africa, have many different criteria for their noun classes. Take the Nigerian language of Fula: it has twenty genders, none of them based on sexual difference, with nouns for human males and human females belonging to the same group.

Keeping things as simple as possible, English has not only binned the masculine, feminine and neuter gender groupings of its Anglo-Saxon days (where violence and power were feminine, girls were neuter and women were masculine), but has also lost almost all the different forms its nouns once had. In modern English, nouns change only when we add an 's', usually to make a plural: one 'boy', two 'boys', one 'aardvark', two 'aardvarks'.

Actually, that's a spelling rule which ignores a distinction we always make though we remain oblivious of it. When we pronounce those 's'es, we use either an 's' sound or a 'z', depending on whether the noun's final sound is voiced (pronounced with vibrations from air coming from the lungs) or voiceless (with no air and no vibration). Voiced consonants like 'g' and 'v' and all vowels, because vowels are always voiced in English, take a similarly voiced 'z' in the plural, whereas voiceless consonants, like 'k' and 'f', take an also voiceless 's'. (Take 'p' and 'b', both produced by parting the lips, the only difference being that we make a 'b' sound with air coming from the lungs and 'p' without. Unknowingly, and ignored by the spelling system, we turn words ending with a voiceless 'p' into a plural by adding an equally voiceless 's', those ending with a 'b' with a voiced 'z' – 'cups' and 'cubz', 'pups' and 'pubz', 'laps' and 'labz'.) Nouns which already end in an 's' or 'z' sound turn plural with an extra '-es' (pronounced '-ez' because there's a vowel before the 'z').

English's happily simple system finds a direct contrast in German, which has eight ways of marking plurals, with seven of those so crazily varied they're basically irregular. Old English originally had at least nine ways of marking plurals, including an '-as' ending which is the ancestor of our 's'. By Middle English, two plural forms remained – '-as' had become '-es' and there was also '-en' – but the '-es' ending prevailed, maybe because it was both easier to hear and to combine with the 's' ending for plurals in Norman French.[5] The 'n' ending survives in several irregular nouns in standard English – 'children', 'oxen', 'brethren' – but there are a few more in some dialects in the north of England and particularly Scotland, where forms like 'een' ('eyes') and 'shin' ('shoes') are still widely used. In *The English Dialect Grammar* of 1905, Joseph Wright recorded lots of weird and wonderful 'n' plurals in many other dialects, but I'd be surprised to hear if they're still around – 'been' for bees and 'tone' for toes in Cheshire, for example, 'ashn' for ashes in Pembrokeshire and southwestern counties, and even 'cheezn' for cheeses in East Anglia and Dorset and 'wopsn' for 'wasps' in Hampshire.

Incidentally, English defines a plural as any number more than one – e.g., 1.00001 litres – whereas French, for example, takes plural to mean a minimum of two (1.000001 litre, deux litres). Both English and French have opted for the binary model of singular + plural, but there are others, most popularly the three-way singular + dual + plural.

No gender categories with separate forms. A straightforward singular–plural operation. The third learner-friendly feature of English's nouns is that they operate a laughably simple case system. In grammar, cases refer to the different forms nouns can take to indicate what is happening to them: if they are doing something or

---

5 Pinker, *Words and Rules*, p. 229.

75

having something done to them; if they are being owned or addressed or if something is going towards them or inside them or lying on them; if they are being placed somewhere or are being used somehow . . . In many languages, nouns signal this additional case information with 'inflections', that is, extra endings or beginnings, or changes to the root form. Those languages which operate case systems for their nouns tend to do so with some gusto, with most having at least six cases. Lak, a language with about 150,000 speakers in Dagestan in southern Russia, has nineteen cases, Kayardild, spoken in northern Queensland, has twenty, and Hungarian has twenty-one.

With singulars and plurals, Hungarian nouns can come in forty-two different endings. But even that is small potatoes compared to Basque, whose nouns come in seventeen different cases, times four for definiteness/indefiniteness and singular/plural, with those basic sixty-eight different forms subject to more changes according to other components of the sentence. By one calculation, with two layers of recursion – where a noun phrase is embedded within another noun phrase within another noun phrase – a Basque noun can have 458,683 different forms, but theoretically it could go into an endless loop of infinite inflections.

Most modern Indo-European languages now operate with a pretty simple case system, in marked contrast to our common ancestor Proto-Indo-European, whose nouns came in eight or nine different case forms.

Faithfully obeying the rule that the simpler the society, the more complicated its grammar, Proto-Indo-European's descendants show a steady and remorseless dismantling of that original case system. Latin had six cases and lost those pretty quickly so that only three different noun endings had survived by AD 300. Latin's direct descendant French has just the one form for all its nouns, no matter what's happening to them. Over in the Germanic branch of Indo-European, there were four cases by the third century AD. By the 900s, Old English had three.[6]

This relentless dismantling of the once rococo splendour of the Proto-Indo-European case system was the cause of great lamentation amongst scholars of the nineteenth century. The German linguist August Schleicher compared the process to a statue that had rolled around on a riverbed until it had been eroded into a smooth, featureless cylinder.

Modern English's nouns now have two case forms: the single variation from the basic form comes in our possessive case (also labelled the genitive), when we add an 's' to indicate, as I'm about to, a noun's ownership. 'The boy kicked the girl's ball' – that apostrophe + 's' does the work which can also be done by a preposition – 'the ball of the girl', 'the ownership of the noun'. This possessive case works so well for us that the prepositional alternative usually sounds stilted. 'The ball of the girl'? Not really. And if the possessor is named, the preposition is usually just not on – 'the plays of Shakespeare' is okay or okayish, but 'the ball of Jocasta', 'an advocate of the Devil' or 'the list of Schindler' aren't.

Unnoticed by most grammarians, English's possessive is also applied to some non-possessing circumstances, including time periods ('in five years' time'), artistic creations ('Handel's Messiah'), and family relations ('my mother's cousin'), where an 'of' construction would be either odd or, particularly with those time periods, impossible.

But apart from adding a possessive 's', an English noun doesn't change form even to distinguish the most basic difference, of either performing the action or having something done to it – i.e., if it is the subject or the object of a statement. In the sentence 'The boy kicked

6   Deutscher, *Unfolding of Language*, pp. 92 and 93.

the ball', the boy is the subject, the ball is the object. Similarly, 'The conman kissed the girl', where the conman is the subject, the girl the object; if the roles are swapped so that it's the girl kissing the conman, the nouns keep the same form.

Nor do our nouns change when they take on a subsidiary role as indirect objects. 'The boy gave the ball a kick' – 'kick' is the direct object of that sentence, 'ball' the indirect one. The indirect object always comes before the direct object.

The nearly case-less simplicity of our nouns comes at the price of confusion, even when English does bother to change the case in the possessive. In the sentence 'The boy kicked the girl's ball', there's no way of telling from the sound of that sentence if there's one girl owning that ball or several girls. Or how about 'The boy kicked Cedric's ball then the girls'? He could be kicking one girl's ball, several girls' ball, or he could be assaulting several girls. And the written form depends on the fiddly business of moving that apostrophe to indicate singular or plural – 'girl's' for one, 'girls'' for more than one.

Although they may seem over-elaborate and their many inflections may be very difficult for adults to learn, case systems do offer distinct advantages of clarity, precision and economy. Because it lacks any sort of responsible case system, English has to take the other options open to human language of specifying what's happening to the noun – by using lots of prepositions (like 'with', 'from' or 'to'), and by depending on word order to distinguish subjects and objects.

Word order is supremely important in English, whereas it was often completely irrelevant in case-filled Latin. Romans could put the words 'puer' (the subject form of their word for 'boy'), 'spheram' (the object form of 'sphera', meaning 'ball') and 'recalcitravit' ('kicked') in any order and it wouldn't make any difference to the meaning. (Or take the first line of Virgil's *Aeneid*: 'I sing of arms and the man' is the usual translation of 'arma virumque cano', but that original translates literally as 'of arms of the man and I sing'.) But in English, nouns have to rely on their location to show their role in the sentence. Change the word order and you change the meaning completely: 'The ball kicked the boy' – it's perfectly grammatical if fairly nonsensical, unless I suppose it was a ball in a cartoon, with legs and feet and anger-management issues.

This fundamental and comprehensive difference between Latin, with its case endings to show who's doing what to whom, and English, relying on word order, accounts for the ridiculous results in traditional grammars which have tried to impose Latin rules on English. It also makes things rather awkward for traditional educationalists and pundits who all seem very attached to the idea that learning Latin offers us an invaluable grammatical grounding: you may as well study Sanskrit for all its relevance to the grammar of English or that of almost every other modern European language.

That all-important word order in English is based on the sequence of subject–verb–object. Which you might think goes without saying. Of course the subject, the instigator of the action, the doer, comes first, then the action, the doing, and finally of course the object, the done to. But there actually is no of course about it. Subject–verb–object may seem to us the obvious sequence, one that is enshrined in nature itself, but it is quite arbitrary. Generally speaking, humans tend to favour putting the subject first, and don't usually kick off with the object, but all the ways of ordering the three basic elements occur and all are equally valid. Actually, the order that seems to come most naturally is subject–object–verb (which was probably the original word order of the earliest languages and is still the most popular sequence). It's also the order that even English-speaking SVO-ers most use when we're communicating by gesture: to ask if someone wants a drink in a crowded pub, point to yourself, then the person, then tip the hand sideways and thumb-first to the mouth.

In a survey of 1,377 languages, the *World Atlas of Language Structures* found the following:

Subject–object–verb (SOV)	565
Subject–verb–object (SVO)	488
Verb–subject–object (VSO)	95
Verb–object–subject (VOS)	25
Object–verb–subject (OVS)	11
Object–subject–verb (OSV)	4
No dominant word order	189[7]

As always with human grammar, there are, even with simple and straightforward English, lots of exceptions to the rules. Or rather rule, because with hardly any case system or gender distinctions, the only opportunity English nouns have to become irregular is with singulars and plurals.

Some of our basic words become plural not by adding an 's' but by changing the root form of the noun – 'foot/feet', 'goose/geese', 'louse/lice', 'man/men', 'mouse/mice', 'tooth/teeth' and 'woman/women'. These are forms preserved from the original Old English, as are 'child/children' and 'ox/oxen', plus in a specialised, usually monastic context, 'brothers' and 'brethren'.

Another exception is provided by the dozen words that end in 'f' in the singular but go into the voiced 'v' form in the plural, spelled

---

7   *World Atlas of Language Structures*, online at wals.info. Prospects are not good for the survival of the four OSVs in the survey. Kxoe has a chance of surviving with around 7,000 speakers in the pocket where Angola, Namibia and Botswana meet, but the other three in the survey (Tobati, the language of the people of Jayapura Bay in New Guinea; Nadeb, spoken by hunter-gatherers in Brazil; and Wik-Ngathana, the language of Aboriginal Australians in north Queensland) have only a few hundred native speakers left and will almost certainly be extinct very soon.

'-ves': 'calf', 'half', 'knife', 'leaf', 'life', 'loaf', 'self', 'sheaf', 'shelf', 'thief', 'wife' and 'wolf'. 'Hoof', 'scarf' and 'wharf' can have either a regular 's' form or irregular '-ves' but others like 'roof' are regular.

There are also a few tricky nouns that don't change form for the plural – nouns for animals like 'sheep', 'deer', and 'fish' and many individual species of fish.

Then again, English has quite a few words which stay in the plural and have no singular form – 'clothes', for example, and individual items of clothing that accommodate two limbs, such as 'trousers', 'pyjamas', 'pants' and 'knickers'. Similarly, bifurcated tools or instruments have no singular form but stay plural – for example, 'scissors', 'binoculars', 'spectacles', 'pliers'. And then there are those other nouns which just are plural – we never feel just one jitter or get up to a solitary shenanigan, fall into one arrear or make only one amend.

Just for good measure, there are also some nouns which are always plural in form but take a singular verb, notably 'news', plus some parlourish games (like 'billiards', 'cards', 'darts' and 'dominoes') and some diseases and illnesses which end in an 's' (mostly olden-days ones like 'mumps', 'measles', 'rickets' and 'shingles', but a more recent addition is 'AIDS').

Finally, some singular collective nouns can take either singular or plural verbs – 'government', 'team', and 'family' – depending on whether the speaker is referring to a collective unit or a group of individuals: 'My family is weird', 'All my family are eccentrics'; 'My team is Accrington Stanley'; 'The team are playing out of their skins'. The names of teams, though in the singular, are treated as plurals – 'Accrington Stanley are relegated', 'England were beaten on penalties'.

Collective nouns are one of the four categories that traditional grammars like to sort nouns into. Other examples of collectives are provided by all the different terms for animal and professional groupings – 'a herd of cattle', 'a gaggle of geese', 'a congregation of worshippers', 'a troop of scouts', and so on. The other three noun categories that grammar manuals usually come up with are proper nouns (the names for people and places, which have an initial capital letter, like Oslo, Oswestry and Oswald), abstract nouns (for ideas or mental states – 'beauty', 'capitalism', 'joy', 'disestablishmentarianism') and common nouns (everything else).

As it happens, abstract nouns and proper nouns do deserve subcategories because they behave slightly differently – they don't take determiners, for example – but there is another distinction that English itself makes with its nouns – whether English thinks the things they refer to are countable or not. English considers that most things can be separated into individual items and counted, but not all, and that some things have to be regarded as an inseparable mass. 'Bread', 'cheese', 'salt', 'information', 'weather' – these belong to the uncountable category, as do abstract nouns. Because they are uncountable, these nouns aren't usually preceded by words which specify a number (including 'a' or 'an'). Nor do they usually have plural forms.

EFL students often make mistakes with their uncountables and countables, because, even if their own languages operate a similar count-versus-non-count distinction, their nouns won't necessarily fall into the same categories as in English. For example, 'furniture' is uncountable in English, whereas French 'meuble' isn't.

Like many languages, English can shift a noun from being normally countable to uncountable if the sense of the noun being made up of individual items gives way to a sense of it referring to a coherent group – this is what has happened to 'data' and is currently happening to 'media', both words taken from Latin in originally plural forms (the singulars being 'medium' and 'datum'), but both having shifted to mean a single, uncountable grouping that takes a singular verb, although that process hasn't quite finished with 'media', which we use as both singular and plural.

Then again, there are lots of times when normally uncountables become countable ('That shop has lots of different cheeses', 'How many beers did I have last night?', 'Two sugars, please'), and countables not ('Would you like some zebra?').

Given such regular shifts between the two categories, it's perhaps not surprising that children seem to muddle up countables and uncountables quite happily – 'I ate two breads', 'There's not much biscuits left' – and take their time about sorting their nouns out and getting the distinction right. But once it is absorbed, that distinction carries the force of a hard-and-fast rule – no speaker above a certain age (ten? nine?) of any English dialect would say, 'I ate two breads' or 'There's not much biscuits left'. (Although, as we shall see, the countable–uncountable distinction is beginning to break down when it comes to the use of countable 'few' and uncountable 'less'.)

Abstract, proper, collective and common – these are the traditional categories of nouns which have been imposed in an attempt to make some sort of order out of the organic gloop of our language. The truth is that trying to define nouns in that way is doomed to failure – a fate revealed by that final catch-all category of 'common' nouns, the words for 'things'.

Ah, things . . . So what is a thing? Philosophers of language have tried to differentiate nouns from verbs by describing nouns as 'entity-specific' and verbs as 'event-specific' . Very like a conversation with an inquisitive toddler who keeps asking 'Why?', sooner rather than later, this attempt to distinguish entities from events comes down to the atomic level – events referring to a rapid change in the structure of the universe, entities to a much more stable part of it: so the boy and the ball remain the same while the kicking of the ball involves a movement of the air's atoms and . . .

But never mind the molecules and the rate of change in the universe. What kind of definition can there be of a word class that can include thingy words such as 'house' or 'car', broader concepts such as 'accommodation' or 'transport' and completely abstract terms like 'beauty', 'injustice' or 'existentialism'?

This is one of those many occasions when traditionalist grammarians, who, like all traditionalists, prefer their reality simple, their categories fixed and their hierarchies solid, have a real problem. The truth is that grammatical categories just don't form neat groups with clear boundaries. Word classes aren't discrete but 'fuzzy'. There isn't a list of defining membership rules for any part of speech; rather, they are organised by family resemblances, by prototypes which form a core element of a category, with other items assimilated to the same category by varying degrees.

Fuzziness is all around us – in nature and in human cultures – and any attempts to impose certainties and unswerving rules are going to come unstuck. There are flightless birds, egg-laying mammals, times of war when states deem it okay for their citizens to commit murder, and an infallible, God-chosen Pope who realised he was fallible and took early retirement. Many people would much prefer it otherwise, but life is fuzzy. So is language.

And another thing. There are lots of occasions when words happily swap classes, particularly in English. Words that are usually adjectives are often used as nouns ('The shock of the new', 'Come on, you Reds', 'Here we see the albatross feeding her young'). Verbs become nouns as gerunds. Any other part of speech can function as a noun – prepositions ('the ins and outs', 'the ups and downs'), adverbs ('Gently does it'), even conjunctions ('And is the third most common word in English'). Likewise, nouns can become verbs ('I've just Googled you') or adjectives ('a Beatles record', 'a Ringo song'). And let's not forget the many combinations known as compound nouns, where two nouns come together – 'van driver', 'High Street', 'coffee cup': grammars never classify those first elements as adjectives but they fill adjectival slots and they behave like adjectives by staying the same in plural forms, to the confusion of non-natives who often have a bash at compounds such as 'waters-bottles' or 'windows cleaners'.

All categories of grammar are fuzzy so, like every other word class, nouns resist the traditional sort of cut-and-dried definition. In fact, grammatical categories refer not to a specific set of pre-labelled words but the jobs which words perform in a sentence. The term 'noun' refers to a function, a role, and when a word takes on that function or role it will behave nounishly – it will be a subject or an object, it might follow a pre-noun word like 'a' or 'the' or an adjective, and it might take a plural form. To quote Steven Pinker's definition, a noun is 'a word that does nouny things'.[8]

---

8 Pinker, *Language Instinct*, p. 106. *Fuzzy Grammar: A Reader*, ed. Bas Aarts et al. (Oxford University Press, 2004), offers an excellent, though strenuously academic, collection of essays on this topic.

who often have a bash at compounds such as 'water-bottle' or 'windows cleaners'.

All this works out at roughly... like everyday word-class nouns exist the H-triggered or of cut-and-dried definition. In fact, grammatical categories refer not to a specific set of pre-labelled words, but the jobs which words perform in a sentence. The term 'noun' refers to a function, a role, and when a word takes up that function or role it will behave noun-ishly — it will be a subject or an object; it might follow a preposition word like 'a' or 'the' or an adjective, and it might take a plural form. To quote Steven Pinker's definition, 'a noun is a word that refers to a noun thing.'

4 Determiners

You may not be familiar with the term but don't be put off by it. Determiners are words that you use all the time and unfailingly correctly. They are the little words that go with nouns to identify them in some way: to indicate where they are, or how many of them there are, or whether they're being referred to in a specific way or a general one.

In English determiners always come before nouns.

the/a/an

The most common determiners are 'the' – known as the definite article – and 'a' or 'an', called the indefinite articles.

'The' is the most used word in English, and for those EFL learners whose own language lacks a consonant made by sticking the tongue between the teeth, it is an immediate and often insurmountable obstacle. Just to make things a bit more complicated for (plucking a non-English-speaking people completely at random) the French, 'the' has two pronunciations – *thih*, the usual one, and *thee*, for those times when we want to emphasise something – 'You mean *the* Paul McCartney?'

But the very existence of 'the' and 'a' (our fifth most used word) can also flummox EFL learners whose first languages don't have articles. 'The' and 'a' may be fundamental components of our language – without them, English sounds to us like a series of vague headlines ('man bites dog', 'boy kicks ball') – but they are not linguistic necessities. Around a third of the 7,000-odd languages currently spoken do quite happily without articles – Russian and Polish, for example. (Which is why Russians and Poles often leave them out when they're speaking English.) And although most European languages do now have them, articles are relatively recent additions. Proto-Indo-European had no need for articles; nor did Sanskrit, ancient Greek or Latin or, indeed, Old English, which had little use for definite articles and no use for indefinite articles at all.

'The' is known as the definite article because it acts to specify a noun – which means that the noun will have been mentioned before ('A suspect was arrested yesterday. The suspect, a 28-year-old man . . .') or the speaker and hearer already know which specific thing is being referred to ('Are you going to the party?') or there can be only one example of that noun ('Fly me to the Moon').

Helpfully, 'the' does not change form, unlike many European languages whose definite articles vary according to the gender of the specified noun or which case it's in or whether it's singular or plural. Spanish has five forms of the definite article and modern Greek and German have six apiece. English has its unvarying 'the', no matter if its noun is a subject or object or possessive or plural: 'The boys kicked all the leisure centre's balls into the pond' – couldn't be simpler.

'A' or 'an' are called indefinite articles because they don't define or specify a noun but keep the reference vague. 'A' is used before consonants, 'an' before vowels. We automatically apply the rule according to the sound of a word, no matter how it is written down: e.g., 'a one-man band', 'a unicycle', 'an hour', 'an MP'.

Since they refer to one thing, 'a' and 'an' can't be used in the plural, where indefiniteness is conveyed by an absence of any article. 'He's a kleptomaniac and that's what kleptomaniacs do'; 'I won't eat a Big Mac because Big Macs are horrible.'

Neither can 'a' or 'an' be used before those nouns, like 'flour' or 'furniture', which English considers to be uncountable. Applying indefinite articles to uncountable nouns is one of the mistakes (the singular verb with 'they' isn't one of them) made by Ali G when he conducted his interview about science with Professor Heinz Wolff:

ALI G: What is the smallest thing in the universe?

PROFESSOR HEINZ WOLFF: The smallest things in the universe are, I should think, some of the elementary particles which make up an atom.

ALI G: How small is they?

PROFESSOR HEINZ WOLFF: Well, how small, I mean, how, you mean in linear, in sort of . . .

ALI G: Yeah, in centimetres.

PROFESSOR HEINZ WOLFF: Ten thousand millionths of a millimetre.

ALI G: Is it smaller than a sand?

PROFESSOR HEINZ WOLFF: [indecipherable]

ALI G: Is it smaller than a salt?[1]

In his next question, Ali G misuses his definite article – 'How is science involved in the medicine?' – because subjects of study, like medicine, history or literature, aren't usually accompanied by any articles. The follow-up question, however, makes no errors, where an indefinite plural means there is no article at all – 'What about knob enlargements?'

Articles are also dropped before proper nouns – i.e., the names of people or places – and abstract nouns. We wouldn't normally say 'the Ali G asked the questions', 'he comes from the Staines' or 'he's really into the self-improvement'.

That at any rate is the general rule but there are many

1   11 O'Clock Show Channel 4, series 1 episode 6, 8 October 1998.

exceptions to it. Only one involves abstract nouns: these can take 'the' when they are used specifically – 'The courage is an enviable virtue' is unacceptable but 'The courage of the soldier under fire' is fine.

Similarly, there are words that can be used with or without articles, depending on whether they are being used to mean something in particular or in a sort-of-abstract, general way – 'hospital', for instance, or 'work', 'prison', 'church', 'bed', 'home'. You can see the difference between the articled and article-less uses in the following pairs: 'She's in hospital – she went to the local hospital', 'They're out of work – they've finished the work on the dodgy electrics'.[2]

Even if their own languages do use articles as much as English, EFL learners often make mistakes with their thes and as, since each language has its own rules about when they can be used or left out. These mistakes with their articles by non-natives will usually be very noticeable because either the grammar will sound wonky to us ('She has a degree in the astrophysics') or the intended meaning will have shifted. Take an example like 'He was voted out of office': insert a 'the' and you no longer have a normal part of the democratic process but colleagues electing to banish someone from their workplace.

Most of the exceptions are to the rule banning definite articles before proper nouns, because we often use 'the' before names, particularly of geographical features – the Amazon, the Severn, the Himalayas. Countries also take a definite article if their names are plural (the Maldives, the Netherlands) or announce their status in

---

2 This rule doesn't apply in many Scottish English and Irish English dialects, where such words used generally can still take definite articles – 'I've got the flu', 'He's in the jail', 'You'll be starting the school soon'. In the very brief grammar section of the *Survey of English Dialects: The Dictionary and Grammar* (Routledge, 1994) (Clive Upton, David Parry and J.D.A. Widdowson), 'the' turned up with ailments in many English dialects too, but the survey dates from the 1950s.

some way (the United Kingdom, the United States, the Democratic People's Republic of Korea). 'The' also turns up if the name follows the formula of adjective + noun (the Great Barrier Reef, the High Street) or noun + of + noun (the Bay of Bengal, the Strait of Gibraltar, and quite a few place names in Scotland, where this pattern seems particularly popular – the Mull of Kintyre, the Yetts o' Muckhart, including one whose consonants manage to bamboozle the French and Japanese alike, the Firth of Forth).

'The' also turns up before the names of works of art and architecture (the *Mona Lisa*, the Empire State Building), hotels, restaurants and hostelries (the Ritz, the Ivy and the Dog and Duck), newspapers (but not magazines – the *Guardian*, the *Little Snippington Bugle* but just *Elle* or *Tramspotting Monthly*), organisations (the UN, the CBI), some services ('You need to call the police. I think it's 999 but you could look it up in the Yellow Pages or on the Internet'), musical instruments ('he's learning the flute'), musical ensembles (the London Symphony Orchestra, The Beatles, the London Welsh Male Voice Choir)[3] and the names of families when families are referred to collectively – the Joneses, the Kennedys, the Flintstones. Both those last two rules apply in the case of The Smiths.

this/that; these/those

These are pointing words, officially called 'demonstratives'. In standard English, 'this' and 'that' are used for singular nouns, 'these' and 'those' for plurals.

---

3   In the early eighties, Matt Johnson called his basically one-man indie band after the definite article – The The, for my money the most tiresome and irritating name of any group ever. The The snarls the linguistic software – 'the' as a noun? what? – so that saying it ('Do you like The The?' 'Are you going to the The The gig?'), even silently to myself ('What's the name of that guy in The The?'), felt, I remember, uniquely unpleasant.

A third of all current languages may have no need of articles, but almost all languages have demonstratives. These pointing words were probably one of the first of the parts of speech to emerge as human grammar evolved – 'no, not this cave, that cave' – and were most likely accompanied by actual pointing gestures. According to one theory, pointing words may have been the source of pronouns ('this' equating to 'I', 'that' to 'you', a further-away pointing word to 'he/she/it'). More obviously, pointing words very often provide the basis of articles – as is shown in the European languages which evolved from Latin, whose word for 'that' – 'ille' – provided Italian 'il', Spanish 'el' and French 'le'. Similarly, our 'the' developed from Old English's 'se/seo/thaet', which were mostly used as pointing demonstratives. ('A' and 'an' developed in Middle English from 'an', the Old English for 'one', just as Italian, Spanish and French took their indefinites from Latin 'unum'.)

'This', 'these/that', 'those'; they form a basic binary system of distance (near and far, here and there). Half of the languages in the world have a two-pronged pointing system like English. About a third have a three-reference system, usually indicating here, there and far away. About 5 per cent have even more refer-ence points. Koasati, a native-American language now spoken by about two hundred people in Louisiana, has a six-strong system of demonstratives – near, near the speaker, near the hearer, far away from the speaker, far away from the hearer, and far away. (Even Koasati's demonstratives are still based on three reference points – the speaker, the hearer, and the thing being referred to. That's as much locating as the human brain seems to need, or can take.)

Old English used to have a three-way system but the far-far away difference was mostly dropped in Middle English. However, there are several dialects which have preserved the original set-up.

Some Scottish English dialects have 'this-that-thon'/'yon' – 'No, not that yin, yon yin ower there.' They're on their way out, but dialects of southwest England used to be notable for their demonstratives, 'thease-that-thicky' – 'If you was to put that stick in across thicky pony.' (My apologies for the example but that's the one given in a study of the demonstrative determiners of South Zeal, a village in Devon.)

many, much, etc.

Another series of words usually classified as determiners are the 'quantifiers', so called because they specify something not by distance, as do 'this' and 'that', but by quantity. The two most basic pairs are 'many' and 'much' and their opposites, 'few' and 'little'. There are two pairs because they apply separately to countable and uncountable nouns. 'There aren't many biscuits left.' 'How much whisky did you drink last night?'

That distinction is also revealed with some other quantifiers – which can only be used with countable nouns, never with uncountables – because they refer, however vaguely or negatively, to a number: 'both', 'several', 'each', 'every', 'various', 'either' and 'neither'.

The countable–uncountable distinction disappears with some other quantifiers. One pair are the comparative and superlative forms of 'much' and 'many', which are 'more' and 'most' for countables and uncountables alike ('Most men are rubbish at multitasking'; 'More tea, vicar?'). Other quantifiers are vague enough about the number to be used with uncountables as well – 'some', 'enough' and the various nebulous phrases that run along the lines of 'a lot/plenty/loads/heaps + of'.

Traditionalists tend to get hot and bothered about the way we often use the opposite comparative pairings – 'fewer' and 'fewest', 'less' and 'least' – complaining about our habit of applying the uncountable forms to countable nouns, as in the supposedly heinous supermarket notice, 'Five items or less'.[4]

Word order is very important in English, not just in identifying the general business of who's doing what to whom but also at the level below that, in sequencing the words within particular grammatical operations. So when two or more determiners appear together they do so in strict order. Some quantifiers such as 'all', 'both', 'half' and 'twice' come before articles and demonstratives ('the', 'a/an', 'this', 'that', 'these', 'those') and numbers and other quantifiers, including 'many/much', 'several' and 'various'. So that we would say, for example, 'I am determined to visit all the many attractions in Skegness.'

Many British dialects used to allow a definite article before 'both', but this survives now mainly in Scotland: 'Labour and Conservative, I hate the both of them.'

which, what

Finally, there are the two determiners used in questions – the interrogative determiners 'which' and 'what', a pair which distinguishes not by distance or countability but, just like 'the' and 'a', between the specific versus the general. Hence the following party enquiries: 'Which colour would you like – red or white?' and the bloke-to-bloke introductory staple, 'So . . . what team do you support?'

---

4   Henry Hitchings explains that this blurring isn't the heinous invention of illiterates at Marks & Sparks but has a venerable history, the result of 'less' and 'least' mirroring the way that the positive forms 'more' and 'most' have been used for countables and uncountables ever since our language dropped the Middle English distinction of 'more' with countables and 'mo' with uncountables. *Language Wars*, p. 288.

5 Adjectives

Definition

Adjectives are describing words – 'a *small* boy', 'a *bouncy* ball', 'a *broken* window'. As in those examples, adjectives usually describe nouns, and in English they almost always come before the nouns. They also turn up in English after 'to be' – 'The ball is bouncy'; 'The window is broken' – and other 'link' verbs: 'become', 'get', 'seem', 'appear', 'look', 'make', 'turn', 'sound', 'taste' and 'smell' – 'He turned nasty', 'he looked terrifying' and 'he smelled awful.'

As with all the word classes, the term 'adjective' refers to a grammatical role rather than a set of specific words like 'small' or 'young'. A word is an adjective when it fills an adjectival slot, describing a noun – 'the X boy'. 'X' could well be 'small' or 'young' or 'remorseful', but it could also be a word we would normally use as a noun – 'the Barnardo's/Borstal/Asbo boy' (delete according to generational preference), 'the kitchen window', 'the Everest double-glazing'. Verbs can also be hoiked into service as adjectives – 'a bouncing ball', 'a miskicked ball'.

Because different kinds of words can also fill noun-describing slots, some grammar manuals classify as adjectives words which I have assigned elsewhere – determiners ('this boy', 'some boys', 'each boy', 'many boys'), possessive pronouns ('his boys', 'your boy', 'their boy') and interrogatives ('which boy?' 'what boy?'). Not to my taste but fair play. There are no fixed categories and a language can be sliced up in lots of different ways. Indeed, in some languages there are no adjectives as we know them, with the descriptive stuff dealt with by relative clauses.

Just as a word that's usually a noun can be an adjective, words which are usually adjectives can operate as nouns: 'The good, the bad and the ugly'; 'Which size would you like? The small, please. Maybe in the pink. Or the purple.'

Form

In a formula that may be starting to seem familiar, adjectives couldn't get much simpler than they do in English – every dialect of English, standard and non-standard alike. Our adjectives don't decline according to case, as they used to in Latin, and they don't have different forms for the gender or even for plurals as they do in French. There they are in all their adult-learner-friendly/child-learner-hostile simplicity – they go before their nouns, probably after a determiner, and they sit there quietly behaving themselves and not getting up to any fancy changes of form.

The only time English's adjectives turn irregular is in the comparative and superlative forms of the basic grading words – following the linguistic Sod's Law which states that irregularities will apply only to the most common words. (Because only irregular words that are used a lot and that are learned early on can survive as exceptions to the regularising rules which children are also acquiring.)

Here is the short list of English's irregular adjectives:

good, better, best
bad, worse, worst
many/much, more, most
little, less least
far, further, furthest

> old, elder, eldest (mainly used with people, as opposed to the
> regular form, old, older, oldest, which can be used of
> everything, including people)

For every other adjective, the comparative and superlative forms are regular.

There are two ways of making comparatives and superlatives in English. One is by simply putting 'more' or 'most' before the adjective, the other by adding '-er' or '-est' to the end, usually of short, one- or two-syllable words. (Standard English prefers 'more' and 'most' except before short one- or two-syllable words, but that's a quirk not a law governed by nature. A quirk within a quirk is that standard English has quite a few two-syllable words that refuse to add on an '-er' or an '-est' and will only take a 'more' or a 'most': following no particular pattern that I can see and for no particular reason – 'bizarre', 'sudden', 'special' and 'precious'.)

Given that English's adjectives really are about as simple and straightforward as a language's word category can be, in a happier, more enlightened world, this bit of the book could quite feasibly end at this point.

However. Because English's adjectives are so uneventful, grammarians have had to make the most of the one occasion when adjectives vary – the comparatives and superlatives. On which they have seized and about which they have set, leaving severe bruising and orders to obey a few rules up which they have just made. The law enforcers have done their job very effectively – some words in the following examples, which are all fine grammatically, are regarded by many as sins, and are all considered definite and basic mistakes in written, standard English.

Old-school rule number 1: You can't add '-er' or '-est' to words longer than two syllables. Well, yes, you can because yes, many of us do – 'the beautifullest woman in the world'; 'an expensiver watch than mine'.

Old-school rule number 2: You can't use both forms together. But again, this has always proved a very popular formula in English – 'the more tastier cheese'; 'the most coldest summer since records began'. In his analysis of dialects of late Victorian times, Joseph Wright noted that 'more' and 'most' were not only used everywhere to intensify comparatives and superlatives that already had '-er' and '-est' forms, 'more' and 'most' were usually used *only* to do so, with almost all adjectives taking '-er' and '-est' (and some dialects of Yorkshire and Cumbria even producing 'badder' and 'baddest', 'gooder' and 'goodest').[1]

But despite this construction's widespread and long-standing use, a traditionalist would red-pencil a double superlative such as 'most coldest', explaining that only one form is needed so the second is redundant and somehow ignorant. Hence the certainty of a grammar guardian such as Craig Shrives who acknowledges that a double comparative or superlative is 'a common mistake' but goes on to explain that it's also 'a grammatical howler', 'pretty unforgiveable'[2]. A 'common mistake'? There really can't be any such thing. If enough people use a particular form then it's part of the language, which is the collective creation of all us individual experts.

In fact, like many languages, English quite happily allows the repetitions in 'more hotter' and 'most quickest' to make the meaning more emphatic, which is why it's used most often with superlatives. The double superlative is not only not a mistake, it has a distinguished pedigree. Let's cite the unimpeachable example of Shakespeare, whose Julius Caesar, when stabbed by Brutus, laments: 'This was the most unkindest cut of all.'

Old-school rule number 3: The comparative form can only be used for two, superlatives for three or more. This is another

---

1 Joseph Wright, *The English Dialect Grammar* (1898).

2 *Grammar for Grown-Ups* (Kyle Books, 2012), p. 114.

invented regulation rather than an actual grammatical rule, because we often use superlatives for two things, with no resulting confusion nor the instinctive objection that greets a genuine grammatical error. 'Brünnhilde is the eldest of my two daughters.' 'Email me or phone, whichever's best for you.' That superlatives for two actually come easily to us explains how they crop up in well-worn phrases, which are always accepted without any spluttering indignation – 'the best of both worlds'; 'may the best team win'; 'put your best foot forward'. Even H. W. Fowler, in the classic grammar and style guide, *Modern English Usage* (first published in 1926), has to concede that correcting these supposed exceptions to this supposed rule (Ah, well, strictly speaking, one should of course say, the better of both worlds, shouldn't one?) would be 'pedantry'. Why, yes, I rather think it would.

Old-school rule number 4: Neither comparatives nor superlatives can appear with absolute or extreme adjectives such as 'perfect' or 'excellent'. This is justified with an appeal to logic – that if something's perfect, for example, then it can't be said to be more or most perfect, as in the cliché about it being impossible to be a bit pregnant.

But we do grade absolutes and extremes, and we might well say that a woman who is a basketball-shaped 39 weeks gone is more pregnant than the woman staring at the blue line on the test she's just bought from Boots. (The law makes just this judgement, grading pregnancy so that abortions are legal before 24 weeks.) Similarly, the emphasising urge that gives us 'most coldest' and 'more tastier' also results in lots of more completes, most perfects, and most evils. Hence too the linguistic inflation we've seen in the percentage descriptions of usually sporting, most often footballing, commitment – it must have once been the highest praise to say that someone had given 100 per cent but nowadays the bare minimum seems to be 110.

The ban on grading extreme words isn't based on some timeless law – it's a fad, a fashion, which doesn't go way back to classical Greece but to a couple of generations ago. Fowler doesn't even mention the problem in the first edition of *Modern English Usage* in 1926, but by 1947, when he produced *Usage and Abusage*, his 'guide to good English', Eric Partridge is judging 'the most excellent fellow of them all' to be 'infelicitous' and any qualification of 'perfect' to be 'inadmissible'.

Because it was a newly minted timeless law, Partridge & Co. had to ignore the examples of previous generations who were quite happy with 'most excellents' and the like. One of the very many weird bits of *Usage and Abusage* happens when Partridge takes the eminent nineteenth-century critic George Saintsbury to task. Apparently, Saintsbury made a bit of a bish with something Partridge calls his 'blended genitives'. The offending example is, 'His versification is by far the most perfect *of any English poet*' – the offending words in italics, with Partridge correcting them to 'of all English poets'. Partridge repeats the sentence with its inadmissible 'most perfect' seven times, offering different versions and analyses, before he finally mentions the elephant in the room at the end in brackets – '(For the further infelicity, the most perfect, see COMPARATIVES, FALSE).'

It's not just the elephant Partridge has had to let his gaze pass over, it's the pink tutu that elephant's wearing and the violin it's playing and the beachball it's balancing on. Because the person making the inadmissible schoolboy error of describing something as 'most perfect' was a pillar of the late Victorian literary establishment, one of the most respected writers of his day, and indeed the professor of rhetoric at Edinburgh University. The kind of man who didn't get his grammar wrong, you would have thought. But Saintsbury's brand of belletristic waffle was very fond of most perfects and most brilliants. 'The sonnet is the most perfect of poetic forms', opines Saintsbury in his *History of Nineteenth Century Literature*, published in 1896. 'Southey has the purest and most perfect English prose style', Carlyle produced 'the most brilliant . . . work in English literature', and Shakespeare wrote 'the most perfect work yet done by any man in literature'. Saintsbury even uses 'very' with extreme words – as when he rates Alexander Kinglake's travel book *Eothan* as 'very brilliant'. Such supposedly false comparatives were once very popular, until the twentieth century, when they were banned, and when, coincidentally, they seemed to fall out of fashion in conversational English. When it's used now, 'very + extreme' indicates a certain strangeness or incompetence, as in the title of a TV comic travel series of 2008, *Keith Lemon's Very Brilliant World Tour*. There are exceptions, of course, notably Californian dudespeak's 'most excellent', but overall it seems that fortunately, for once, the rule-makers have made up a rule which happens to agree with what's really happening in the language.

Rules

Our adjectives may be simple but they do come with rules. There aren't many of these rules but they are sometimes sophisticated and often stern so they present problems for adult learners. We, however, remain happily unaware of them. The real rules of English's adjectives are as follows.

Rule number 1: Participles. In all varieties of English, adjectives can be formed from the present ('-ing') or past ('-ed') forms of some verbs (labelled the present and past participles). However, their meanings are different, sometimes obviously, sometimes subtly. Adjectives with the '-ing' form are active, having some sort of effect on the universe, and those with '-ed' are passive, on the receiving end of something doing the effecting – if someone is amusing, boring, interesting or frightening then you will be amused, bored, interested or frightened.

There's a potential difficulty here; how to tell the difference between an '-ing' word that's a verb working as an adjective, and an '-ing' word that's a verb working as a verb. 'He is being boring' – adjective. 'He is boring me' – verb. 'He is boring on and on' – verb. 'He is boring' – either: he could be a bore or someone engaged in some sort of engineering works. One test is to try a qualifying word like 'very' in front of the '-ing' word: if 'very' works, the word is an adjective; if it doesn't make sense, it's a verb. Interestingly, although children can make errors like 'he is very boring me', they have to be very young children and such mistakes are soon corrected, indicating that although we're unaware of it, we get to grips with word classes and syntax early on.

I have noticed just one occasion when an adult native speaker has managed to get an '-ing' verb-or-adjective confused – the native speaker being Freddie Mercury, the occasion being one of the daftest of all the daft lines in 'Bohemian Rhapsody' – 'Thunderbolts and lightning, very, very frightening ME'. Couldn't that first 'very' have been an 'are' and the second a 'really' or something? Actually, couldn't the whole line have been completely rewritten? The entire song, ideally.

Rule number 2: Some adjectives can't be used after verbs like 'to be' or 'to become' and can only be used before nouns. Examples are 'chief', 'former', 'future', 'main', 'principal', 'sheer' and 'utter'. A few adjectives are normally used only after verbs like 'to be' – 'glad' and 'well', plus a group of others all helpfully beginning with 'a-': 'abroad', 'adrift', 'alike', 'alive', 'alone', 'ashamed', 'asleep'. And others can appear before nouns and after verbs but with a change of meaning, notably 'bad/good', 'big/small', 'heavy/light', and 'early/late'. 'I caught a very late train so thank goodness it wasn't late.' 'He's really thin for such a heavy drinker.'

Rule number 3: When two or more adjectives appear in a list, they do so in particular order. It really has to be 'the big yellow lorry', 'a little black dress', an 'itsy, bitsy, teeny, weeny, yellow, polka-dot bikini'. English is not weird like this – it seems that the way adjectives are ordered is broadly the same in a large number of languages, possibly reflecting the way different areas of the brain are involved in itemising such sequences.[3]

However, note that 'broadly'. The precise ordering varies from language to language, so this is one of those areas of grammar where adult learners face enormous problems in grasping really complicated rules which we have at our unconscious command. So complicated are these rules that EFL manuals offer a marvellous variety of different categories and orders and in doing so often get themselves into a bit of a tizz. I pity the poor learners faced with our adjectival sequences as explained in one of the standard EFL textbooks, Thomson and Martinet's *Practical English Grammar*, which takes over a page to outline its separate categories and the order it's putting them in, and which I still find, after a lot of stumped gazing, pretty baffling. 'Several variations are possible,'[4] say the authors, in an immediate admission of defeat, 'but a fairly usual order is: adjectives of (a) size (except **little**; but see C below) (b) general description (excluding adjectives of personality, emotion, etc.) (c) age, and the adjective **little** (see B) . . .' The eyes relax, the mind slips out of focus and the day's earworm – 'Little red Corvette', perhaps, or 'itsy-bitsy, teeny-weeny, yellow polka-dot bikini' – starts up.

This is, broadly, the sequence of different types of adjective in English:

---

3 See Stephen Nadeau, *The Neural Architecture of Grammar* (MIT Press, 2012), p. 110.

4 A.J. Thomson and A.V. Martinet, *A Practical English Grammar* (4th edn) (Oxford University Press, 1986), p. 35.

Opinion	Size	Age	Shape	Colour	Origin	Material	Purpose
silly		young			Italian		
	big	old				wooden	mixing
beautiful	large	old	round	black	Japanese	metal	baking

We often vary this order without raising too many eyebrows, especially when we're making a long list. But when non-natives fail to follow the usual adjectival sequence, we notice and register it as a proper, fully fledged mistake. 'I very much like your London red big buses,' observes the English learner and we blink away a smile.

Colours

The words which make up the fifth element in that sequence seem fundamental, archetypal adjectives. They definitely are to my six-year-old son whose homework the week before I wrote this was, conveniently but I swear coincidentally, to make a list of describing words. 'Oring, yelow, red, purlpe,' he wrote: 'blakc, wite, gry, blue, green, turkwoise . . .' Ten of the twenty-three words in his list of describing words were colours.

We tend to think of our senses as losers in the animal kingdom. Cats can see better in the dark than us, and dogs have a hugely superior sense of smell. But in fact humans enjoy one of the most developed systems of colour vision on the planet, a trichromatic system, with added focus on the yellow-green parts of the spectrum. This evolved in primates about 30 to 40 million years ago when they acquired the mutation of an extra gene that added a third group of cones in the retina. These cones were particularly sensitive to yellow and proved very useful in helping our distant ancestors distinguish ripe yellow fruit from the surrounding greenery; a development which, as Guy

Deutscher points out, turned primates into the bees of tropical fruit trees.[5]

So we humans have always had the same top-of-the-range colour vision. Cro-Magnon caveman stalking a gazelle and twenty-first-century child doing his homework on the computer, commodities traders on Wall Street and Piraha hunter-gatherers in the Amazon rainforest, we have all seen the same bright rainbow.

What then to make of the strange colour words in the oldest works of literature? Take the colours of the first and still the most revered poet of European civilisation, Homer, whose most famous phrase is 'the wine-dark sea'. Actually, the word Homer uses to describe the sea is 'oinops', which translates directly as 'wine-looking'. The wine-looking sea . . . – an arresting description, it's true, but it can't be the magnificent poetic licence of an un-pin-downable genius because it's not really meant to be at all arrresting; it's one of the customary phrases used in oral poetry as familiar landmarks for the audience and the memory-stretched reciter and it really shouldn't have such a weird flourish.

Various explanations have been given for Homer's puzzlingly winey sea: Greek wine could have looked green or blue in some lights; the sea might have looked reddish at sunset, Homer was as blind as a bat. But eighth-century-BC Greek wine came in the same colours as it does today, and the sea he was talking about was the same azure-blue Mediterranean as today's, the only difference being that it was full of fish instead of carrier bags and the shards of old lighters. And to make matters that little more confusing, the only other thing that Homer describes as 'oinops' is an ox. He also uses the word for the flower violet, 'ioeis', to describe the sea, which might be slightly nearer the mark, except that Homer also uses 'ioeis' to describe iron.

---

5   Guy Deutscher, *Through the Language Glass* (Arrow, 2011), p. 247.

Even if Homer was one blind man and the *Iliad* and the *Odyssey* were all his own work, rather than, as seems more likely, epics which were possibly by one man but one who was refining and reworking into a culmination already existing tales which had been recited and added to from one generation to the next, could someone not have helped him out and suggested a tweak to his winey sea? But apparently nobody did. So how on earth could Homer and his ancient Greek public think that the Mediterranean looked like wine?

The answer is – because this was the eighth century BC and 'blue' didn't exist yet. That also explains why Homer never mentions the colour of the bright Mediterranean sky. And it's not just blue that's missing in Homer; he does very occasionally use words that would later denote yellow and green but very, very confusingly.

It's not just Homer. There is no blue in the Old Testament (composed mainly from the sixth to the third centuries BC) or the Indian Vedic epics (composed between 1,500 and 500 BC). And, like Homer, who could describe honey as green, the Bible manages to come up with green gold.

It seems that in those BC years ancient Greek, biblical Hebrew and the Sanskrit of the Vedic epics had only three definite colours – black, white and red. Yellow was the next to appear, then green, and blue was the last of the primary colours to be specified.[6]

It's a process that's revealed in the different colour terms of languages that are spoken today. Of the 119 languages analysed by the World Color Survey, 10 still had just three colour categories – black, white and red or occasionally a red/yellow composite. Interestingly, these languages – like Mündü, spoken by about 25,000 people mainly in South Sudan, or Kuku-Yalanji, whose

---

6 I've tried to find out when each colour word first appeared but I don't think there's any research that's been done on this. Please write to me if I'm wrong – I'd really like to know.

240 speakers live in the rainforest of far-north Queensland – are all spoken in the tropics: the further from the equator, the more colour words in the language. Just under half the languages surveyed had at most five colour categories – usually black, white, red, yellow, and one grueish, bleenish word for green and blue. Hunched in the rain, far from the equator, English belongs to the 10 per cent of languages that have eleven colour categories – black, white, red, green, yellow, blue, brown, purple, grey, orange and pink.

Homer had just three. He saw the same rainbow as us, as did the people who wrote the Bible and created the ancient Hindu epics, as do the speakers of Mündü and Kuku-Yalanji. However, like them, Homer didn't have words for the rainbow's contents. He could talk in terms of lightness or darkness but not specific colour. Homer could do shade but not hue.

Colour words, which may seem so basic and essential to us, are not natural, inevitable, necessary components of a vocabulary. For all but the most recent of the several hundred thousand years of our species, humans have talked quite happily with only black, white and red on their vocabulary palette. That colours aren't the obvious, no-brainer necessities we may think they are is indicated by the struggle many toddlers have to name them.

The thinking is that languages define colours as humans make them: colours have been added as dyeing technology has progressed. Red is the easiest colour to make – red-ochre paint pots have been found in the Blombos caves in South Africa that are estimated to be 100,000 years old, and words for red probably have a similarly ancient history. Yellow and green are the next easiest colours to make, and usually the next colours to appear in a language's vocabulary, followed finally by blue, the hardest colour to manufacture.[7]

---

7 There is a terrific account of the evolution of colour terms in Deutscher's *Through the Language Glass*. Rather brilliantly, Deutscher bases his acccount on the prescient research

In 1969, Brent Berlin and Paul Kay published a very influential study, *Basic Color Terms*, which claimed that all languages added the same colour terms in the same order, and that this was a universal pattern which was clear evidence of some innate workings. They identified seven stages in this universal colour-vocabulary expansion: 1, dark/black, light/white; 2, red; 3, green or yellow; 4, green + yellow; 5, blue; 6, brown; 7, purple, pink, orange, grey.

There have since been disputes about their research, but it does seem that Berlin and Kay's sequence holds good, mostly if not universally, and it is mostly backed up by the World Color Survey.[8] But this needn't be because the acquisition sequence is prewired or 'natural' in some way. Maybe dyeing technology's progress tends to be the same, or maybe the sequence reflects some feature of the visual systems in our brains.

We tend to assume that colours have certain meanings: blue for boys, pink for girls, white for innocence, black for mourning, and so on. But in South Africa, the colour of mourning is red, which in China is the colour of good luck and wedding dresses, and which in ancient Egypt meant evil, death, anger, the desert and victory, and which for us carries equally varied meanings from danger to love and from communism to Stop!

Red was also once taken to be the colour of fiery manliness, which is why pink was proposed as the best colour for boys early in the twentieth century. Blue was suggested for girls, because that was the colour of the Virgin Mary. Actually, there were no firm associations of any colour with either gender until the 1950s, which is when our apparently timeless boysy blues and girly pinks were invented.

---

of the amateur Homerist and future prime minister, William Gladstone, who pointed out the wonkiness of Homer's colours – and was completely ignored.

8 There's a particularly vigorous attack from Geoffrey Sampson in *The 'Language Instinct' Debate*.

Since then, pink has also become the colour of the gay movement, a reclaiming which cites the pink triangle that identified homosexual men in the Nazi prisons and concentration camps. The Nazis seem to have selected pink at random; that there was nothing essentially effeminate about pink for the Nazis is surely demonstrated by their choice of pink flags for their panzer divisions.

A few years ago, researchers at Newcastle University claimed to have detected some indications that women might prefer colours away from the blue end of the spectrum. But this is, at best, a very, very general preference and not one that supports any notions that blue somehow has to be the colour for boys. If that preference does exist, it is easily overriden by culture, as the many, many meanings of redness show.[9] Our colour coding is not enshrined in nature.

Opinions

Cuckoo clocks, yodelling, Toblerone, discreet banking for criminals – Switzerland has given the world many things, but it hasn't been known as a hotbed of radical ideas since the Reformation. Except for one extraordinary period at the start of the twentieth century, when two Swiss citizens produced in the same year two of the greatest ideas of the twentieth or any other century.

The first was created by Albert Einstein, a young German who had taken Swiss citizenship and who was working in the Swiss Patent Office in 1905 when he offered the world his special theory of relativity. Then in 1916, when he was a professor at Zurich University, Einstein applied the same ideas to gravity and created the general theory of relativity.

---

9   Anya C. Hurlbert and Yazhu Ling, 'Biological Components of Sex Differences in Color Preference', *Current Biology* (21 August 2007).

That same year saw the publication of a far less celebrated but also momentous, groundbreaking work by a professor at Geneva University, Ferdinand de Saussure. The book was *Course in General Linguistics*.

It was a posthumous publication. Saussure had died, at the age of fifty-five, three years before, without actually having written the book. In fact, he'd been not writing the book for several decades. He'd brought out his first book when he was twenty-one – a precociously brilliant analysis of Indo-European, which at a stroke solved a long-standing puzzle about Proto-Indo-European's vowel system. Following this triumph, he had an illustrious academic career, teaching Latin and Sanskrit and the history of Indo-European. But he didn't publish anything. Even when he developed his astounding new ideas, although he did make several attempts, he couldn't write a second book. Instead, he delivered his thoughts in three series of lectures he gave at Geneva University between 1907 and 1911.

Having delivered his lectures, he then destroyed all his outlines and rough drafts. So Saussure didn't actually write *Course in General Linguistics*. In fact, he'd done his best not to write it. Or even not to have it written for him. He had left behind very little by way of manuscripts or even notebooks, anything at all that could be cobbled together for publication.[10] *Course in General Linguistics* had to be compiled from their notes by some of the students who'd attended those lectures. (Fortunately, they took excellent lecture notes.) So this is a book in form only, not written by its author but reconstructed from the memories and interpretations of members of the audience at what were to-whatever-extent-unscripted performances.

---

10 Eighty years later, a cache of Saussure's manuscripts was discovered in the orangery of the family home but these show him tentatively working his way towards the ideas which he stated more confidently in his lectures.

Reading the book even now, a century on, it's easy to see why Saussure's students scribbled down every word they could during those lectures, and why they went to all the bother, so inexplicably rare amongst university students, of reconstructing those notes in book form, and getting them out into the world.

First, Saussure surveyed his own subject, noting that the linguists of the nineteenth century had been mostly devoted to detailing the history of individual words, mainly of the Indo-European family whose tree they had discovered. From now on, he stated, scholars should have a much broader remit, to study the ways words work within languages, their sounds and systems and meanings. Saussure had completely redefined Linguistics.

Next, he completely redefined reality.

He did this by analysing the status of words. We may tend to think of words as the names of things but, Saussure pointed out, they are not. Words, he explained, are actually symbols, 'signs'. These signs have two component systems: the sequence of sounds that forms a particular word, and the things these words refer to. Or rather, more precisely and more breakthroughingly, not the things themselves but the idea of these things. The word 'tree' doesn't have a one-to-one association with a particular tree; it's a general, symbolic reference to the concept of a tree.

Saussure went on to observe that the relationship between the word and the concept is arbitrary. There's nothing in the word 'tree' that makes it the inevitable term for a tree, no essential treeness about that combination of vocal sounds that qualifies it for its meaning in English, any more than there's anything in French's 'arbre' that makes that the natural word for one of those things with trunks and branches and leaves. So 'tree' and 'arbre' and all the other words in every language have no inherent, essential meaning. They gain their meanings solely from their context, from their status within the structure of the language they are part of. Eureka!

It might not sound like a Eureka! insight, but it really is. As Saussure said, 'its consequences are numberless'. This is because exactly the same applies not just to words and languages but to all kinds of signs and symbols in society. Things which we tend to think of as natural – pink for girls – are actually man-made constructs with no basis in reality, their meanings derived only from their place within an equally arbitrary system of such signs – blue for boys, white for innocence, red for danger . . .

Saussure proposed that Linguistics should actually be but one branch of a much broader discipline, which had yet to be created, called semiology, studying the use of signs in society. (In the United States, C. S. Peirce was reaching similar conclusions from a starting point in logic rather than language and christened the subject 'semiotics'.) Saussure envisioned that semiology should be able to analyse with quasi-scientific objectivity the workings of artifical systems of symbols – 'rites, customs, etc.'

Whether or not Saussure fully appreciated what this entails, we'll never know, but that 'etc.' actually means 'everything'. The implications of Saussure's insight are much greater than realising that pink for girls is not natural. The subsequent status rejig, from unquestionable part of the natural order of things to contingent item within an artificially created system, applies to every human creation, not just language and clothes but all our abstract creations as well, our beliefs, values and judgements. Every thread of the fabric of our thinking, our culture and our society is 100 per cent man-made.

We may think that pink is for girls or fish is for Fridays, or that democracies are better than dictatorships, but none of these notions has any inevitability or necessity about them. They can find no more justification for their existence in reality than 'tree' can be taken to be the proper word for a tree. They are not enscribed in the code of Mother Nature herself but are made up by humans. Just as 'tree' does, they acquire their meaning from their relationships within the systems that have created them.

It's not a difficult proposal to grasp, unlike Einstein's theories of relativity, but this relativism has clearly proved very difficult to accept. Saussure's revelation did indeed inspire many – the twentieth century saw profound re-evaluations of various academic subjects, notably anthropology and cultural studies, by the semiologists and structuralists who applied Saussure's relativist insight. It also chimes loud and clear with the century's social movements for democracy and against the traditional hierarchies and exclusions.

But Saussure's breakthrough has failed to make the impact it should have done, and is yet to revolutionise our everyday thinking, because it is radical, and because it does demand a complete rethink, as big a rethink in its way as looking up at night and seeing unimaginably distant suns rather than a sparkly roof to the sky. Certainly, sixty years after he gave his lectures, when I was studying English Literature at university, his relativist principles had yet to dawn on any of my teachers or any academic writing I came across. The firm, unquestioned orthodoxy was still in fixed qualities and hierarchies; there was good literature, which was good for you, bad literature which was worthless or even damaging in some way, and all of it was quantifiable, with assignable places in the Eng. Lit. league tables. Shakespeare always occupied the top spot in the Premiership, Milton was almost always in second place, maybe Wordsworth was at number three, George Eliot number four . . . all the way down to 'trashy' pedlars of paperback nonsense languishing in the Evo-Stick West Berkshire Third Division (South).

Of course, football league tables do actually measure reality. Whether by luck or its lack, the teams in those tables have played games with real, quantifiable outcomes, summarised under the columns marked 'W' 'D' 'L' 'Goals F', 'Goals A' and 'Pts'. But there's nothing measurable about Shakespeare, nothing that anyone can say makes him the best, or better than Milton or Wordsworth . . . or better than any writer. Even Barbara Cartland. It would be feasible to claim, 'Usain Bolt is the best 100-metre runner on the planet' because that can be backed up with reference to his world-record times. But 'Usain Bolt is the best runner on the planet' is a personal opinion, unprovable and eminently arguable, and quashable, were Usain Bolt ever to race in a marathon. Unless they are substitutes for other measurable adjectives such as 'fastest' or 'most successful', 'best', 'better' and 'good' are personal opinions about human creations, subjective terms with no reference to any external, objective measuring stick. 'Shakespeare is better than Barbara Cartland' is an empty statement – 'better' at what, exactly? With a gazillion titles to her name, Barbara Cartland was evidently much better than Shakespeare at churning out Mills & Boon romances. 'I think Shakespeare is better than Barbara Cartland' – that statement, though, is perfectly acceptable, if not overly interesting.

Whenever we leave the realm of the measurable, of scoreboards and stopwatches, we find ourselves in the completely subjective territory of entirely human judgement – and that's where 'good', 'better', 'best', and all the other adjectives of that first 'Opinion' column belong. 'New York is bigger than York' – okay. 'New York is better than York' – I can see where it's coming from but it's still only an opinion, as valid as the other point of view from someone who hates big cities and adores cathedrals, railway museums and Viking-era city centres. Whenever someone uses judgement words, like 'good' or 'bad' or any of the other weasel opinion words like 'beautiful' or 'wrong', as though they were delivering unarguable facts, they should be greeted with two awkward questions: 'Why?' and 'Says who?'

*

I hope today's students have more enlightened teachers, but I don't see any sign of that in my own booksy world. I still see books being assessed as though the judgements were in some way objective, as though there is such a thing as 'good' and 'bad' work, as though there are still natural divisions between different kinds of books and certain literary books are just 'better' than the rest.

This failure of relativism to be widely accepted dawned on me a couple of years ago, when I tried out my literary league tables schtick on a friend who is astonishingly well informed about lots of subjects and scarily intelligent. So I was fairly confident that I'd be on safe ground in mentioning the daftness of Eng. Lit.'s Premiership and how it wasn't possible to say, 'Shakespeare is better than Barbara Cartland'.

My friend laughed. No, he didn't just laugh. He guffawed. Starting with a proper spluttering bark. He threw back his head and slapped feebly at his thigh, helplessly overwhelmed by the hilarious idiocy of what I'd just said – a piece of wishy-washy, relativist nonsense, the literary equivalent of political-correctness-gone-mad daftness. Shakespeare! Not better than Barbara Cartland! Ahahaha. Ahahaha. A-hahahahaha.

If it's hard enough to rethink aesthetic judgements along relativist principles, then it has been even more difficult with other human creations, particularly morality. Awkward truth it may be, but 'good' and 'bad' have no reference to or grounding in external reality in our moral judgements, just as they have no league tables to refer to in literature. Nothing is inherently, essentially bad or good – these are our assessments, our labels and our concepts.

We may not have a language instinct but we certainly have at the very least a strong predisposition for absolutes, as well as for accepting given realities as just that. Even in the clearly unfixed areas where semiology has prospered, like fashion, we treat given reality as proper and real, all other possibilities as maverick or silly. I have lived through the Beatle cut, the middle-parted feather cut of the 1970s and the brushed-forward Caesar cut of the 1990s; each time the new hairstyle has become the norm, turning the fashion it has replaced into a mockable anachronism. Or look at the way that people have carried jumpers they're not wearing. In the 1970s it was an acceptable, actually rather smooth, practice to sling the jumper over the shoulders and tie the arms together in front, a method that would these days excite derision among the young almost everywhere outside some golf or yachting clubs, now that the new norm has been established, of wearing the jumper round the waist. There's nothing inherently silly or better about either method, of course, but it doesn't feel like that.

By a not particularly delicious irony, one of the areas where relativist attitudes have made no impact is on popular thinking about language. Unquestioned criteria are applied unquestioningly. Our use of our language is still deemed 'good' or 'bad', 'pure' or 'vulgar', in accordance only with social prejudice. 'My grammar's better than yours.' 'That's not good English.' 'That's bad grammar.' Why? Says who?

The insights of Ferdinand de Saussure, it seems to me, complement the latest findings of the discipline he founded, because both reveal the same fundamental truth: that there are no essences.

There are no essences in human culture; there is nothing that has to be so, no human creation that is written in nature. Whether it's a political system or a religious faith or a pink dress for a little girl, there is nothing absolute, natural or unquestionable about them. They are all as man-made as 'tree', BBC 2 or the International Space Station.

There are no essences in our heads, either: we have no innate attributes; we don't have souls. Our minds are created by our brains, the product of unimaginably intricate networks of neurons. As our neural networks grew, so did our memories, our abilities, our language, our sense of our selves. We are our own creations.

6 Pronouns

Definition

Pronouns are words that can stand in for nouns. Like most determiners, their primary function is to cut corners by replacing nouns or whole noun phrases that don't need to be repeated. 'The boy wearing the Barcelona strip kicked the ball that was splattered in mud and Idontknowwhat' – 'He kicked it.' But even with less long-winded sentences, 'He kicked it' will save on usually at least two words and very often quite a lot of words. Pronouns are very, very useful and we use them a lot, slightly more than nouns, in fact, in conversation.[1]

Their very close relationship with them has led pronouns to be reclassified by some modern grammarians as a subcategory of nouns. I've restored them to their own chapter because . . . of vague personal preference. Based on the gut feeling that pronouns just aren't nouns – the way they inflect, their refusal to be accompanied by determiners or adjectives ('Did the you go to the shops?' 'Check out the beautiful her.').

Very unlike nouns, pronouns don't have fixed meanings. Pronouns are function words, like determiners, with only grammatical significance, acquiring specific meaning according to their context and the nouns they're referring to. When I say 'I', I mean me: when you say 'I', you mean you, if you see what I mean.

---

1   Douglas Biber, Stig Johansson, Geoffrey Leech, Susan Conrad and Edward Finegan, *Longman Grammar of Spoken and Written English* (Pearson Education, 1999), p. 235.

Also unlike nouns, some of our pronouns have retained the ability that all nouns once had in Old English of changing form according to case. As we shall see, this causes a HUGE problem.

There are various types of pronoun – relative, interrogative, whateverative – which will appear briefly at the end of the chapter, most of which is going to be about the main category, the personal pronouns.

Here they are in standard English:

Subject	Object	Possessive with a noun	Possessive instead of a noun	Reflexive
I	me	my	mine	myself
you	you	your	yours	yourself
he	him	his	his	himself
she	her	her	hers	herself
it	it	its	its	itself
we	us	our	ours	ourselves
you	you	your	yours	yourselves
they	them	their	theirs	themselves

Most other languages have more, often many more, entries in their tables of pronouns, especially along the top line if they have any sort of case system. Here is the table for just the third-person pronouns in case-and-gender-inflecting Old English:

	Singular			Plural
	Masculine	Feminine	Neuter	
Nominative	he	heo	hit	hi
Accusative	hine	hi	hit	hi
Possessive	his	hire	his	hira
Dative and instrumental	him	hire	him	him

The blurring of the instrumental and dative cases shows that Old English was already beginning to prune some of its flourishes, but since Middle English that tendency has grown into the firm policy with our pronouns, as with the rest of the language's syntax, of ever-greater simplicity. Standard English has managed to drop the case difference with 'it' and 'you', with 'you' also remaining unchanged for singular and plural (apart from the reflexive, 'yourself' and 'your-selves'). So few are the forms that they can be confusing, especially with only 'you' for one or many.

Standard English used to have different forms for the second person – 'thee/thou' for the singular, 'ye' or 'you' for the plural. Just as it still does in French and in fact the majority of our neighbouring European languages, the plural was also used for one person in respectful or formal contexts – an Elizabethan would automatically say 'Your lordship', 'thy Lordship' being an unthinkable combination of words – just as using a 'tu' must still be to a French employee addressing the CEO.

(These different forms of the second person in most other European languages have had to undergo a readjustment with the development of democracy. The more familiar forms are increas-ingly popular in all but obviously respectful contexts, and when respectful forms are still used they must now be reciprocated. Gone are the days when the peasant would address the landowner with a formal plural and be given a casual singular in return. Recently, the French have also been grappling with the new phenomenon of its younger citizens using only 'tu', particularly on Facebook and Twitter. Not just its younger citizens either: Nicolas Sarkozy caused a bit of a rumpus when he ran, success-fully, for President, using only 'tu' forms, to intimates and strangers alike. The French elite do not like change, especially in French, so the use of a 'tu' to a stranger – quite a friendly little tic, you'd have thought, and nothing to get steamed up about – has got them steamed up. The journalist Laurent Joffrin, for example, has described the habit as 'a form of violence'.)

In standard English, in the sixteenth and seventeenth centuries, the 'thou' form became reserved for either cosy intimacy or a fairly aggressive expression of social superiority, as the plural 'you' began to spread – until 'thee' and 'thou' had become quaint, homely forms of broad dialect, gradually dying out throughout the language. Today 'thee' survives as an intimate form in some dialects of northern England, but even in its old heartland, the southwest of England, it probably won't be around for much longer.

Unlike standard English, many dialects have addressed the problem of singular and plural 'you/you' for one and more than one, keeping 'you' in the singular but amending it to mark a plural – 'youse' in Irish, Scottish, some American, and northern English dialects and, in many southern states of the USA, 'you all'. Although 'youse' now turns up in many different British dialects, it seems to be an Irish import, and a twentieth-century one, judging by its entry in Wright's *English Dialect Grammar* of 1905 – it's a 'curious form', notes Wright, found only in Ireland and, oddly, parts of Norfolk.

Another oddity of standard English crops up in the reflexives, which are all based on the form in the third column, the possessive subject, apart from 'himself' and 'themselves' where the reflexive is based on the object form in the second column. Most non-standard English dialects don't have this irregularity and base their reflexives on the third column throughout to produce 'hisself' and 'theirselves'.

These dialect forms make perfect linguistic sense yet they are regarded at best as quaint and usually as wrong, and they would certainly be marked in red pen on any official or public document.

To repeat. There is no linguistic basis whatsoever for the downgrading of the dialect variations. 'Youse told him to do it hisself'

– that's a completely valid, entirely grammatical statement with no mistakes in it, no corruption or laziness: on the contrary, the dialect version could reasonably be considered preferable to the standard English equivalent with its confusing singular-or-plural 'you' and its irregularly formed reflexive.

As our pronouns show, standard English is not better, somehow more linguistically proper or more sophisticated than any other dialect of our language. Standard English is one dialect amongst equals, but it has been prized over other dialects, which have been duly mocked and derided as wrong when they vary from the standard, only because standard was the dialect spoken by the people who had the power to make it standard.

With the exception of those that have an additional 'youse' or 'y'all', all non-standard dialects of English have a pronoun table with the same structure as standard's. However, there are many, many different dialect forms of many items in that table. Here for example are the first-person plural pronouns of working-class Glaswegian English: 'we, us, wur, wurs, wurselves' Whereas standard English has 'I, me, my' in the first-person singular, in working-class Tyneside dialect, that declines, perfectly validly of course, as 'I, us, me' and in the plural the equivalent of standard's 'we, us, our' is 'us, we, wor'. So working-class Tyneside, like many other northern English dialects, has 'us' in the first-person singular as an object and as the plural subject but not as the plural object as it is in standard (which in Tyneside English is 'we') – 'Give us back me ball.'

Many other dialects have that possessive 'me' instead of standard's 'my' ('I'll get me coat') and many in the north of England have 'us' where standard has 'our' ('We're having us tea'). Some rural – i.e., rapidly vanishing – dialects from central England, and some American dialects, have possessives from column four that end in '-n' – 'mine', 'yourn', 'hisn', 'hern', 'ourn', 'yourn', 'theirn'.

However, the dialects with the most distinctive pronoun table are those of rural – i.e., rapidly vanishing – southwest English. In some dialects, even the basic structure of southwest English's pronoun table differs from that of standard and of other non-standards. The best-known example is 'thee' in the singular. Less well known is the odd third-person singular – in Somerset English, the masculine and feminine forms ('she', 'her', 'he', 'him' or 'un') are used for inanimate nouns instead of the neuter 'it' – with the twist that these nouns have to be of countable things – sugar, love, etc. can't be replaced or referred to by 'he' but a chair or a vase certainly can be.

On top of animacy–inanimacy and countable–uncountable distinctions not made by other dialects, rural southwestern English also has a complex system of what has been labelled 'pronoun exchange', where the object and subject pronouns regularly swap places – 'Give it to he', 'Her don't take sugar', 'Her just biffed I on the nose'. However, this process isn't invariable, being governed by strict if pretty well impenetrable rules, mostly based on emphasis. 'We went there, didn't us?' is acceptable, for example, but 'Us went there' is ungrammatical. I think. And it's not just me who's uncertain. The pronoun exchange of southwestern dialects has baffled those few linguists who've studied it: 'We are not yet entirely sure how this operates', admit the editors of one of the very few books on dialect grammar.[2]

Then again, standard English has its own system of pronoun exchange, which is just as baffling. It involves only those pronouns which change form according to their case, i.e., whether they're the subject or the object of a sentence. 'I/me', 'he/him', 'she/her', 'we/us', 'they/them'. Perhaps because we're so unused to having to deal with case inflection, they behave very oddly.

---

2 *Dialects of English: Studies in Grammatical Variation*, ed. Peter Trudgill and J. K. Chambers (Longman, 1991), p. 9.

The oddness happens as soon as there's a conjunction involved. 'Well, between you and I . . .' 'Me and him, we were the ones who did it.' 'Her and me have always been close.' 'You'll be cooking tomorrow night,' the presenter Gregg Wallace warns the contestants on *Masterchef*, 'not just for Michael and I but three esteemed restaurant critics'.[3]

They might seem strange, exposed in the cold light of print, and indeed object–pronoun exchanges with a conjunction join the list of things that keep subeditors employed by newspapers and copy-editors by publishers. They're high up that list because they come naturally to English speakers of every dialect, standard and non-standard. They have a long and distinguished history, being noted as a feature of all British dialects by Joseph Wright, and indeed were busy swapping cases in the fifteenth century.[4] Yet they seem on consideration to be clearly grammatically wrong. 'Between you and I' – what's a subject pronoun doing after a preposition? 'Me and him . . . did it', 'Her and me have always been close' – these are object pronouns acting as subjects, and that first example originally even has a subject 'we' immediately replacing the objective 'me and him'. Interestingly, it is the mistake most made by English-acquiring toddlers, but even infant-school children would never say 'Me was the one who did it' or 'Her has always been close' – so clearly, obviously, the correct, grammatical formulation is 'He and I, we were . . .', 'She and I have . . .'

But almost all English speakers do swap their object and subject pronouns around, even the poshest and correctest of us. The only people I've heard use the supposedly correct form have all been professionally employed as users of correct English – teachers, subeditors, people in publishing . . . they do say things like 'She and

---

3   *Masterchef*, BBC 2, 15 November 2012.

4   In *A History of English Syntax* (Holt, Rinehart & Winston, 1972), Elizabeth Closs Traugott notes its use by Caxton and others in the fifteenth century, throughout England.

I went to the shops' – sometimes, when they remember to – but faced with a conjunction, everyone else doesn't – 'Her and me have always been close.'

In fact, sometimes, the conjunction really demands an object form – 'I and she have always been close' doesn't seem acceptable; if you're going to start that construction by referring to yourself, you really have to use 'me'. One grammar guardian has tackled this head-on and he has stuck to his logical guns – 'If you refer to yourself first, the same rule applies. It's not "Me and Jim are going . . ." but "I and Jim are going"'.[5] Really? In all honesty – 'I and Jim are going . . .'?

Can that really be right when it sounds so wrong? Why does it sound so wrong? Are we all wrong? How can we all be wrong at our own language?

We're not wrong because we can't be; it's our collective linguistic behaviour which defines the language we speak. Unless, I suppose, we aren't all grammatical geniuses but are all capable of basic errors. It's odd that we'd all make the same basic error and it runs against the basic premise and all the findings of modern linguistics but it is a possibility, that our subject–object pronoun exchanges could be just us all floundering about on the only occasion we're ever presented with case marking and making a right old hash of it.

Another explanation restores us to grammatical geniushood. This states that in these 'Me and him went' constructions we're actually functioning with our customary intuitive expertise. What we're doing when we say things like 'Between you and I' or 'Me and him went' is following a grammatical rule that kicks in with conjunctions. In 'He went to the shops', the single pronoun behaves normally, taking a subject form in a subject position. But with 'me and him', it's the whole phrase which is the subject, and the component pronouns

---

5 Paul Brians, *Common Errors in English Usage* (Hoffman and Leisy, 2003).

are freed from grammatical responsibility. 'Strictly between you and I, it was me and him who went to the shops.'

I'm not entirely sure about that. It's born of a conventional, old-fashioned Chomskyite analysis, citing such unicorns as the subjacency constraint. But I think the conclusions are broadly right, and it's certainly bang-on about the dominance of object forms in our pronouns. It seems to me that many people use subject pronouns ('I', 'we', 'he', 'she', 'they') only as subjects and only when they are the sole subjects. Certainly, for most of us, our default seems to be the object pronoun – with items of a subject phrase linked by a conjunction ('Me and Jim'), after link verbs ('It's me', no matter what the grammar fiends would have you believe), and on its own ('Me! Me! Me!').

However, there's another factor at work here complicating matters – the etiquettey, proper-grammary stipulation that it really should be 'taller than I' or 'It is he', and that, technically speaking, we should be using subject pronouns in comparatives and after link verbs. These are actually completely artificial rules, invented by the grammarians of the eighteenth century, but applied extensively since. Actually, in English grammar, in both examples there should be object forms – 'She's taller than me'; 'It's him'. Of course.

However, coupled with uneasiness about 'Me and him went to the shops' structures, the non-rule rules about 'taller than I' and 'it is he' have managed to assert themselves. So much so that subject pronouns, especially 'I', have come to be seen, by some, as the 'correct' form, everywhere, always, in object uses as well as subject. These people use subject pronouns whenever they can in a policy of manic hyper-correction – 'She's smarter than he', 'We British . . .', 'Everyone but he laughed a lot', 'Briony said that the youngest, namely she, should go first'. I recall a well-heeled acquaintance telling her son off about his pronouns when he told on his sister and added, 'but that's between you and me'. 'You and I, darling,' his mother corrected. 'Between you and I.' Hence, too, David Cameron's pronoun in his chatty explanation about government policy – 'What drives Nick Clegg and I . . .'[6] Actually, there are two competing explanations for that 'I'. One is that David Cameron was swapping his subject and object pronouns because they were freed from grammatical responsibility; the other is that he is posh.

Subject pronouns have also become, for some, a mark of correctitude, one of the grammatical shibboleths that sort out those who are washed and those who are not. As the Chomskyite linguist who analysed the errant subject pronouns earnestly explained, the 'Prestige Usage' was 'grammatically deviant' but had been applied by the man nonetheless: 'the attempt at maintaining PU by prescriptive grammar and the education system leads only to a linguistic tool for maintaining instead socio-economic class barriers. Those with access to advanced education and paid secretarial services can effortlessly intimidate, confuse and disorient those without such access.' (The essay was published in 1986, which seems a modern enough date to me, but those 'secretarial services' do place it in the olden days. So, granted, things may have loosened up a bit grammatically since 1986. Not that I've noticed.)[7]

But the prescriptive rules are up against it. Rewrite 'Me and Mrs Jones' or 'Me and my shadow'. Or the first phrase of a line which then hyper-corrects in Roxy Music's 'Virginia Plain' – 'Me and you, just we two, let's get into something new'.

---

6 Quoted in the *Guardian*, 16 July 2012.

7 Joseph Emonds, 'Grammatically Deviant Prestige Constructions', in *A Festschrift for Sol Saporta*, ed. M. Brame et al. (Seattle: Noit Amrofer, 1986), pp. 93–129.

we

Pronouns acquire their meanings purely from their place within their pronoun table, so it is perhaps surprising that they do have a tendency to change their position. Even 'we', the most stable of our pronouns, can shift, in particular circumstances.

The first happens in the very specific context of the patronisingly chummy enquiry by a medical professional – 'How are we feeling today?' 'How are our stiches?' 'Is our MRSA on the mend?'

'We' can also mean 'I', but only for the monarch – and only in official documents. When she speaks, the Queen never uses the royal 'we'. Neither did any of her recent and not-so-recent forebears – including, it seems, Queen Victoria, who always used normal 'I's, 'me's and 'my's. On the one occasion when Queen Victoria did use 'we' in her famous catchphrase – 'We are not amused' – she was speaking at a dinner party, and was probably doing so on behalf of the entire table, in response to an equerry who'd just ventured to entertain the party with a risque piece of gossip – an equerry still sublimely unaware that he was about to suffer one of the most shaming put-downs in history.

The royal 'we' has been used in various languages. It spread throughout Europe in courtly Latin in the fourth century AD, rulers latching on to its presentation of themselves as somehow embodying, personifying the nations they controlled. The royal 'we' arrived late on this island: the first king to use a 'we' for an 'I' in England was Henry III (1216–72). (Another pronominal development in the Middle English courts was plural 'you' beginning to be used as a singular to the monarch and others of higher rank.)[8]

I can think of only one occasion when a standard-English speaker

---

8 This historical snippet comes from Traugott's *History of English Syntax*. Who was the last monarch in Britain to use the royal 'we' and mean it? My guess is Charles I, the last king to think that he really had been given the job by God.

used 'we' as a singular – on 3 March 1989, outside 10 Downing Street, when Margaret Thatcher announced, 'We have become a grandmother of a grandson called Michael' . There are two possible explanations for that curious glitch. (1) After one word of her brief statement, Margaret Thatcher mislaid all memory of either the syntax of her original sentence – 'We are' + e.g., 'delighted to announce . . .' – or, after three words, her husband. (2) She'd just heard about the birth of her first grandchild! She was prime minister! Announcing the birth of her grandson to the nation! At that moment, at one of the great peaks of her life, the magnificence of it all got to Margaret Thatcher and propelled even her syntax into the regal. At that moment, in her head, she might as well have been – no, she was – the queen.

It only lasted for that moment. In her next reply to the press corps' clamouring, she used a conventional pronoun – 'I've spoken to them and their baby's well'. In the answer after that, she does go back to using 'we', but by now surely she's referring to Denis as well as herself – 'The only sorrow is that we shan't be able to see the baby. But we hope to see some snapshots soon.' 'We've got a grandson, it's marvellous.'

you

As well as doubling up in standard English for both the singular and the plural, 'you' also moves up the pronoun table with some ease, often turning up as a first-person pronoun, meaning 'I' or 'we', shading into an inclusive impersonal like French's 'on' – as used twice in quick succession by Margaret Thatcher during her grandmother proclamation – 'It's something very deep within you. You know, to have a grandson is just a wonderful thing.'

'You' in this sense turns up in our idioms a lot – 'you know', 'you never know', 'you try and you try and you try . . .' It's also freely available in everyday conversation – 'Can you get a decent wi-fi connection in Stornoway?' 'You always know England are going to lose on penalties.'

'You' has been used as the narrative pronoun a few times. In Jay McInerney's *Bright Lights, Big City*, the narrator addresses his slightly younger self, the 'you's maintaining a suitably arch and smart feed-back loop of self-involvement. Mohsin Hamid uses 'you' very interestingly in his novel, *How to Get Filthy Rich in Rising Asia*, where the 'you's start out as inclusive, helping to make the main character a type, supposedly exemplifying the lessons of a novel which presents itself as a self-help guide to business success. As the book develops, the nameless 'you' becomes an individual being addressed, and then, in a hospital scene, to startling effect, the reader, or at least that's how I read it, and it really was startling.

he/she/it

This trio of pronouns are the only words in English which follow a gender system. And not just a two-way gender system but a three-way gender system, the whole masculine–feminine–neuter set-up which goes back to the Bronze Age and Proto-Indo-European. (Their three genders seem to have evolved from a two-way animate–inanimate system, the animate half subdividing into male and female.)

As so often in life itself, the straightforward gender distinction in English grammar comes up against a few problems. One of those is the inability of the 'he/she' pronouns to cope with situations where the gender of the person being referred to is unknown or irrelevant. 'It' would be the obvious solution, and the one taken by many languages, but in English, the neuter 'it' is firmly non-human and unusable in referring to people. The one exception is newborns, when the sex of the human is of secondary importance to the fact of its existence – used, as it happens, by Margaret Thatcher as she continued in her grandson announcement : 'Each baby, any mother will tell you, they're not just like one another, each baby when it's born has its own personality, its own character.'

Often, as Margaret Thatcher does once in that sentence, we adjust by opting for the gender-free plural 'they' (see below) – 'Each baby . . . they're not just like one another'; 'Everyone has their price.' More finickily, another option was to provide both alternatives – 'Everyone has his or her price.' The simple convention used to be to use the masculine for both – 'Everyone has his price'. The masculinist 'he' continues confidently enough in some set phrases – 'He who hesitates is lost' – but it has become not really acceptable, in normal conversation as well as in print, to use the lordly 'he' for both genders. It's a tiny detail of change within the grammar but it is the symptom and product of a profound cultural shift. And one that happened very quickly. I'm guessing that the culture's attention was first drawn to the inherent sexism of the all-encompassing male pronoun in the early 1970s. So, from out-there-polemic soup to cultural-norm nuts – just forty years.

The trouble is that we haven't had time to find a replacement for the seigneurial 'he'. One attempt was made by 'one' but that proved irretrievably posh. Although 'they' is popular as a gender-unspecific alternative to 'he or she', it's used most often in conversation, because in print the plural form as a singular can look a bit odd and even naive. One solution in written, particularly academic, English was to come up with a new amalgamated, sexless pronoun, such as 's/he'. (This subject form seems bad enough but the others are worse; dutiful and cumbersome – 'his/hers', 'himself/herself', etc.) A more popular tactic since has been to alternate the gender of the pronouns between sections, so that one paragraph might have 'he' and 'his', the next 'she' and 'her'. That seems to me the most sensible solution, but I have to admit that I still notice it, and notice it as a slightly forlorn if well-meaning device, whenever I come across the alternating tactic on the page.

it

'It' is a curiosity, a sole surviving remnant from a long-gone era, like the coelacanth. 'It' is a descendant of Old English 'hit' – as 'it' is still pronounced in many working-class Scottish dialects – but 'it's ancestry is much older than that. As the only words with a neuter-gender marking, 'it', 'its' and 'itself' are the last three surviving forms in our language of the three-gendered, masculine–feminine–neuter noun system operating in Proto-Indo-European five and a half thousand years ago.

As well as referring to a neuter thing, 'it' also has a grammatical function, when it steps in to help out with the structure. In this function, 'it' is meaningless – 'semantically empty' is the harsh judgement of the *Oxford Modern English Grammar*, which distinguishes four uses: referential 'it' (when the noun is known – 'The boy kicked it'); dummy 'it' (when we're talking about our surroundings – 'Gosh, it's warm today'); anticipatory 'it' (for situations when 'it' stands in for a longer phrase later on in the sentence – 'It is obvious that he's a complete and utter nincompoop'), and cleft 'it' ('It is the Prime Minister who is to blame', 'It was the Sun wot won it').

one

As well as a gender-free singular for humans, standard and, I think, all dialects of English have also lacked that singular's availability as an impersonal pronoun, like French 'on' or German 'Man'. The sign in a French tourist shop will say, 'On parle français'. In the unlikely event that any British tourist shop would have such a sign, it would claim, dubiously, 'We speak French'.[9]

Various pronouns have to be co-opted into filling the gap in English – general 'we', the unspecified 'you' meaning us in general, the sexist 'he' and the singular 'they' in the third person. But the lack of an impersonal pronoun has remained.

Presumably impressed by the success of 'on' in French, some speakers of standard English tried to introduce 'one' as a first-person-singular-cum-impersonal pronoun. That combination and its irretrievable poshness counted against 'one' from the start – there was always a very unwinning aspect about the assumptions and presumptions involved in 'one', which gives first-person state-ments an air of unquestioningly universal application ('Of course, one always goes to Gstaad for a week's ski-ing'). Even so, 'one' still had a degree of success. For some time, the middle class deferen-tially went along with posh 'one' or at least didn't protest, and some middle-class speakers even tried it out for themselves. Here's Margaret Thatcher, the grocer's daughter from Grantham, having a go at using a 'one' in her announcement: 'So many of one's friends are grandparents, but there's just something very special about it'. Even in 1989, a 'one' like that was noticeable, as democracy began to affect the culture and the language, after an interesting delay of pick-your-number-under-five decades. By now, 'one' as a pronoun survives, just, in the way that dialect forms of the verb 'to be' cling on in isolated rural villages. So doubtless there still are pockets of Knightsbridge or the odd Oxbridge college where one can talk about oneself as one without one coming across as awfully affected,

9   In French, 'on' is used a lot, not just as impersonal but instead of all subject pronouns, and it completely replaced the first-person plural 'nous' several hundred years ago – 'on va à la plage' a French person would say, never 'nous allons à la plage' (McWhorter, *Power of Babel*, p. 244).

but out in the real world it has proved increasingly unacceptable, an upper-class quirk to be met with distrust or derision, the grammatical equivalent of fox hunting or wearing bright-red corduroy trousers.

they

Pronouns don't change much. They might have slight shifts of function and some of them might gradually disappear, but as a word class they're usually closed, resistant to additions or completely new forms. That's why they featured so prominently in the study of core words that gave our first and second-person pronouns an ancestry of at least 15,000 years.[10]

So 'they' is unusual, being a fairly recent addition to our pronoun tables, borrowed from Norse to replace Old English's 'hie', turning up in the north where Scandinavian settlers made most linguistic impact, and spreading south, with 'their' also accepted in the south in the fourteenth century and 'them' in the fifteenth century.[11]

'They' is also odd, in the way it can switch into the singular. 'They' has been doing this for 500 years, but it's still usually unnoticed, and is sometimes covert. It's the common choice if we're talking about one person but we don't know which sex he or she is – 'Someone has left their pen'; 'I suppose everyone's entitled to their own opinion, but . . .'; 'The caller has withheld their number.' The singular 'they' is particularly useful where the phone is involved – when, for example, there's a hang-up: '"Who was that?" "They didn't say. Maybe they'll text me."' Sexless singular 'they' is so useful that we've invented a new reflexive form for it – 'themself'. 'Not everyone who is handed a scalpel considers themself a surgeon', runs the example from the

10 See Pagel et al., 'Ultraconserved Words'.
11 Traugott, *History of English Syntax*, p. 137.

Guardian quoted in the *Oxford Modern English Grammar*, 'and not everyone given a Steinway considers themself a concert pianist'. (Begging the bolshie question, how many people are ever given a Steinway?)

'They' also turns up as a singular in a much more intriguing situation – when the speaker knows the sex of the person they – for instance – are talking about but wants to avoid saying which sex the person is, usually because it's incriminating, usually because it involves sex in the carnal rather than the grammatical sense. If you hear someone referring to someone else as 'they', and the speaker knows which gender that someone else belongs to, it's odds on that hanky-panky is on the agenda. 'I'm meeting someone later. They said they'd be outside Cafe Rouge.' Aye, aye.

I once worked with a woman who was conducting a top-secret affair with a married man. Because she refused to tell us his name, he acquired a nickname, 'They', since that's how she referred to him. In her desire to conceal his identity, she concealed everything about him, including his maleness. 'They came round to my place last night,' she'd confide, with a meaningful nod. 'Wife and veg'll be away at the weekend so I've arranged to see them on a Saturday night for once.' 'They told me they loved me but they can't leave the wife and veg just yet.'

That was paranoid discretion taken to a daft extreme. However, 'they' is often used much less daftly to hide a sexual partner's gender. Let's hope that this usage is in steep decline, because it's almost always used by gay people to conceal a same-gendered partner. Consider this grammatically discreet example from a great (subjective status for a personal opinion) song by Joan Armatrading: 'Cause I've found the perfect someone / Who could take me in their arms and love me.' Joan Armatrading still maintains a dignified silence about her private life, and she was even more reluctant to do anything like outing herself in the early eighties when she wrote 'Heaven', so she had to find a way of talking about her lover without revealing that this person might not be a he but a she. And Joan Armatrading managed to do just that, rather brilliantly. The 'someone' and 'Who' are both sexless, and the plural in 'arms' helps to disguise the oddness of 'their' referring not to two limbs but one person.

myself, yourself, etc.

The reflexive forms in that fifth column of our pronoun table on page 120 have two opposing functions; one that adds emphasis ('She said so herself', 'Paul McCartney himself was there') and one that acts grammatically, without emphasis, when it refers to the subject or object ('He went by himself', 'God, he really loves himself'). The emphatic form was around in Old English, but the grammatical form arrived much later, in early modern English. It was still optional in Elizabethan times. We'd have to use reflexive pronouns in the following examples where Shakespeare uses the object form: 'Thou art so fat-witted with . . . unbuttoning thee after supper' says the prince to Falstaff (*Henry IV Part One*, Act 1 Scene 2), and Hamlet's dismissal, 'Get thee to a nunnery'. [12]

Much more recently, our reflexives have acquired a couple of extra uses. One is as a case-safe alternative during any fraughtness about whether or not to use a subject or object pronoun – 'that's between you and myself'; 'Alan and myself then proceeded to the ahem gentleman's club . . .'

Maybe the second use has been around for a long time or maybe it actually is as new a development as I think it is, but whatever its pedigree, it's now a commonly used feature of our reflexives to work as de-emphasisers, turning down the volume on a subject or object

---

12 Deutscher provides an insightful account into the development of the reflexive pronouns in *Unfolding of Language*, pp. 297–9.

pronoun position.

I first properly noticed this muted reflexive in 2000 during the first series of *Big Brother*, when Craig Phillips confronted Nick Bateman in one of the greatest-ever (personal opinion, not a definitive statement) showdown moments on reality TV. Craig started the confrontation with this announcement: 'I'm very disappointed in yourself'. After that, Craig – and Nick and all the other housemates – used normal 'you's, but in that first sentence Craig evidently judged that a bald 'you' would have been too direct, too much of a finger jab at the face, so he pulled his grammatical punch with a 'yourself' instead, his reflexive pronoun revealing the decency that would make him the deserved winner of the first *Big Brother* series.

I recently heard a first-person plural reflexive during a phone conversation with a stranger who reassured me that this was a bona fide call and not some dire pestering about my software or energy supplier. 'You have a broadband account with ourselves,' he said, with much more propriety than an 'us' could have given.

But the plural is much less common than the singular in the first person, because of its use as a sign of self-effacement, normally an individual activity. However, the self-effacement of a 'myself' can be suspect. I really don't know how modest the constant 'myself's are of the DJs on little, local radio stations. These stations are far too small to run ads, so, as they do on Radio 1, the DJs advertise themselves instead; however, not wanting to be caught talking about themselves all the time, they talk about themselves all the time but cunningly rarely using an 'I' or a 'me'. 'Another hour of banging choons from myself, Darren Bloke . . .' 'Big night coming up at Whispers in Acton – on the decks, Scotty B, Darren Bloke and myself, Scotty P.'

It surely takes more than a reflexive to put that right. A first-person pronoun is still a first-person pronoun, after all. Me, myself and I – none of them words you particularly want to hear from a dullard.

Those are the personal pronouns. There are also some other sets of words that are usually categorised as pronouns.

Reciprocal pronouns   'each other/one another'. Like reflexives, they can't be used as subjects.

Indefinite pronouns   A tribute to the human urge to classify, indefinite pronouns come in nine subcategories in the *Oxford Modern English Grammar*. Here, for all indefinite pronoun completists, they are: *additive* ('another'), *degree* ('few', 'less', 'little', 'many', 'more', 'much'), *disjunctive* ('each', 'neither'), *distributive* ('each', 'every', 'everybody', etc.), *existential* ('any', 'some', 'something', etc.), *negative* ('none', 'nothing', 'nobody', 'no one'), *positive paucal* ('a few', 'a little', 'several'), *sufficiency* ('enough'), and *universal* ('both', 'all', 'anybody', etc.). So now you know the difference between an existential indefinite pronoun and a positive paucal one. That might come in handy one day.

Interrogative pronouns   The fancy name for the 'wh-' question words when they're used on their own. 'Who said so?' 'What did he say?' 'Why on earth did he say that?' If they come with nouns, then they're interrogative determiners – 'Which way did he go?' 'What programme did you watch?' ('Where did he go?' and 'What did you watch?' – interrogative pronouns.)

Demonstrative pronouns   The term given to the determiners 'this', 'that', 'these' and 'those' when they appear on their own. 'This will be the last time.' 'Those were the days'. 'That's life'.

Relative pronouns   'who/whom/whose/which/that'. These turn up at the start of relative clauses, i.e., phrases which provide extra information: 'this is the ball that he kicked', 'and here's the window which he broke'. Our rule now is that 'who' is used for people, 'which' for animals and inanimate things, but that wasn't always the case. See the opening of the Lord's Prayer – 'Our Father, which art in Heaven . . .'

Traditional grammars have invented two rules with relative

pronouns. One is that 'whom' must be used as the object form with people, so just as we are supposed to say, 'To whom am I speaking?', we are also supposed to use the actually archaic form in sentences like 'he is the boy whom I blame for the window'. Fowler notes that 'who' is sometimes used instead of 'whom', even in published prose, 'giving the educated reader a shock'. Fowler's example is from an unidentified but evidently hapless newspaper report: 'As Mr Bevin reminds those who in other circumstances we should call his followers...'. 'That is a mistake that should not occur in print,' admonishes Fowler. With such support, 'whom' has clung on in official, written English, but I have noticed recently 'who' replacing 'whom' as an object pronoun even in books.[13]

The second rule is for my money the most difficult to follow of all the traditional rules. Like the rest of them it's a piece of nonsense, but it does exist as an official rule – about the different clauses introduced by 'which' and 'that'. Let Fowler explain, with all the elegance and ease of grammatical correctitude: 'The two kinds of relative clause, to one of which *that* and to the other of which *which* is appropriate, are the defining and non-defining.' In other words, 'that' is supposed to go with defining relative clauses, i.e., ones which, ah, define something that's gone before – 'The film that I saw', 'Here is the ball that the boy kicked'. 'Which', Fowler is passionately convinced, should only be used for non-defining relative clauses, i.e., ones which don't specify their antecedents but provide extra information about them: 'And then after the lottery win we got a free holiday in Florida, which was nice.' A kicker coming in the stipulation that 'which' constructions need to be separated by commas ('The ball, which I'd just given to the boy as a birthday present, broke the window').

The 'which–that' rule has proved unfollowable for just about

13 For example, Terry Pratchett's novel *Dodger* (2012), p. 146, has 'who' for 'whom' in 'It was a rotten thing to do to Benjamin who he knew...'

everybody, and 'whom' is too old-fashioned to make a fuss about, so the only proper shibboleth in the relative pronouns is 'what'. This may have originated in East Anglia but it has spread widely and is often used in many dialects as the relative pronoun where standard has 'which' or 'that'. One thinks, inevitably, of Ernie Wise's reliable boast about 'the play what I wrote'. 'As' also crops up in some Midlands and southern English dialects as a relative pronoun – as in 'the woman as does' – an equally noticeable non-standard marker.

7　Verbs

Just like nouns, verbs in English are about as simple as human verbs ever get. English has a maximum of five forms of each verb, and some verbs like 'cut' have just three. Latin had 120. Kivunjo, a Bantu language spoken in Tanzania, has about half a million possible forms of each verb. Korean has six different sets of verb endings according to the politeness level of the interaction and the speaker's relationship to the addressee. Welsh grammar makes verbs change consonants according to case, possession and governing pronoun in a superbly complicated system. Piraha varies the verb forms according to the witnessing of the actions, with three different endings for 'hearsay', 'deduction' and 'observation'.[1] Yagua, spoken by about 6,000 people in northeastern Peru, has different endings for five levels of remoteness in its past tenses. English has two. English verbs vary according to three grammatical categories – person, number and tense – where the Sino-Tibetan language Chintang has eight and Koasati, spoken by the Coushatta Native American tribe in Louisiana and the current record holder, thirteen. English verbs are, by comparison, a doddle.

Like most English grammars, this one categorises our different verb forms by their different 'tenses'. But, strictly speaking, this isn't quite right. In fact, strictly speaking, English verbs have just two tenses: the past and the present. For one thing, linguists can claim that English has no future tense because our verbs don't change form

---

1　Everett, *Language*, p. 289.

but rely on other, auxiliary verbs – 'will', 'shall', 'going to' – to indicate action after now. As for most of the other constructions outlined below, they are said to indicate different aspects rather than tenses; the difference being that tenses locate actions in time and aspects describe the nature of that action, whether, for example, it has been completed or not or happened constantly or not.

Simple present

The simple present is aptly named. In standard English it is formed by using the stem, the root form, of the verb, except in the third-person singular, which adds an 's'. Here, in persistent tribute to that boy and his ball, is the simple present of the standard English verb 'to break':

I break	We break
You break	You break
He/she/it breaks	They break

Many non-standard dialects have an even more straightforward simple present. Some, like the traditional East Anglian dialects, keep the stem form of the verb throughout, with no additional 's' for the third-person singular: 'He go to work'; 'It always rain a lot on bank holidays'; 'She get blind drunk every Canaries home game.'

Much more common is the non-standard formula of adding the 's' throughout: 'So I tells it to her straight, I says . . .'; 'You loves ice-cream, innit?'; 'We stays there every summer'; 'They never pays their taxes.' (Noticeably with the third-person plural, the +'s' form is often used by non-standard speakers only when the subject is a pronoun. When the subject is a noun, the verbs often take an '-s'-less form, as in standard. For example, 'Amazon and Google never pay their taxes.')

Only four verbs are irregular in the simple present. They are the four verbs which we use most: 'to have', 'to do' and 'to say', which in standard English take slightly different forms in the third-person singular (the vowel change masked by the conventional spelling in 'does' and 'says') and, of course, 'to be', the most irregular of all, and the verb with the most variations in non-standard dialects, such as the regularised 'is' throughout the singular and plural.

However, there are far fewer and less exotic non-standard forms of 'to be' now than there once were. There are five and a half double-columned pages devoted to dialect versions of 'to be' in the *English Dialect Dictionary* of 1898 – an entry which, Joseph Wright noted in his preface, 'cost very considerable time and trouble'. Among the variants recorded are east Kent's 'I are' and 'we am', east Yorkshire's 'is' throughout the singular, Suffolk's 'be' throughout singular and plural, west Berkshire's constant 'be' except for the second-person singular, 'thou beest' . . . and so on and on.

Fewer and less exotic they may be nowadays, but non-standard variants from the standard forms are always conspicuous, so here, for non-standard speakers, is how standard's 'to be' declines:

I am	We are
You are	You are
He/she/it is	They are

Present continuous

In all dialects of English, this is formed by the present tense of 'to be' + the '-ing' form of the main verb, known as the present participle. Here, for example, is the standard version of the present continuous of the verb 'to live':

I am living	We are living
You are living	You are living
He/she/it is living	They are living

Non-standard varieties of English have two opportunities to differ from the standard version; in the pronunciation of the main verb, with some dialects replacing the nasal '-ing' ending with a non-nasal 'n', and of course in the auxiliary verb, with many dialects supplying their own forms of 'to be' – 'I be eating', 'you is having a laugh', 'they is going crazy'.

The continuous '-ing' form is a relatively recent addition to our grammar. It began to turn up in late Middle English, in the fifteenth century, borrowing that '-ing' ending from the gerund (the noun form of a verb, explained on page 180). Because it's a recent rule, there are no exceptions to it, no irregulars, not even 'to be', which combines with itself as an auxiliary and declines just like every other verb – 'Don't worry – Ezekiel's just being his usual rude self'; 'I'm not being funny but he's being really stupid.'

The existence of our two present tenses often stumps EFL students whose own language has just the one form of the present. The usual way of teaching them the difference between our two present tenses is to say that we use the present continuous when we talk about events that are happening right now, whereas we use the simple present for actions that occur usually or most of the time – 'I eat lots of fruit and veg but I am currently working my way through a bucket of fried chicken'; 'She's snogging him because she always falls for weirdos.' 'I'm making toast' – at the moment, right now. 'I make toast' – that's a weird and very dull job description or a strange lifestyle statement. 'You're wearing odd socks' – now, and probably by mistake, the result of a dark bedroom and an unseeing rummage in a shambolic sock drawer.

'He wears odd socks' – all the time, because he's a bit of a prat and that's one of his little things.

That's the usual distinction between the two tenses, but more specifically, we use the present continuous for usually temporary actions but ones that may have started at some undefined point in the past and may continue into the future, so that the notion of the present may not mean the specific moment in space–time that is now but a longer period that includes now – 'I am teaching myself Swahili', 'He's going bald.'

You can see the differences between the two present tenses in the examples below (you can although many a hapless EFL student certainly will not):

I live in Bristol.	I am living in Bradford.
You live well.	But you are living beyond your means.
He lives like a pig.	Even though he is back living with his parents.
Janet lives with John.	Julia is living with Jim.
It lives behind the fridge.	And it's still living there, despite the caustic soda.
We live in a caravan.	We're living in a tepee for charity.
You live for the opera.	You are living in a right old mess with that flood damage.
They live life to the full.	They're living it up in Ibiza.

You can decode a lot about people's feelings by the way they use the two present tenses. 'I live in Bristol' – that's a straightforward statement, with no side to it. But what about 'I am living in Bradford'? Doesn't that conjure up an image of someone who happens to be living in Bradford after living in other places and who probably won't be living in Bradford for good? Now look at the two women in the table. Janet, who lives with John, surely sounds like she's in a much more committed relationship than Julia the flibbertigibbet, who is merely living with poor, imminently heartbroken Jim.

There are quite a few verbs which don't normally turn up in the continuous '-ing' forms but stay in the simple present. These are mostly verbs which describe states (such as 'belong', 'consist' and 'contain') or some sort of emotional or mental activity (e.g., 'adore', 'believe', 'forget', 'hate', 'know', 'love', 'realise', 'remember' and 'understand'). (Using the '-ing' forms of verbs like 'know' or 'think' in the present continuous is one of the noticeable quirks of some Indian English-speakers' English.) Even when describing momentary, temporary events, these verbs will tend to stay in the simple present – 'I love your haircut'; 'I realise I'm being unfair but . . .' However, there are lots of individual, particular exceptions to that general rule. 'Think', for example, is often used in the continuous but never when an opinion or assessment is being given or requested. 'What are you thinking?' is okay, especially between young lovers, but 'What are you thinking of the new James Bond film?' isn't. 'Feel' can easily turn up in the continuous ('I'm feeling a bit peaky') but not when it means 'think' ('I feel it's for the best') or is used as a link verb – 'Your skin feels so soft'. That list of exceptions is getting longer – take the McDonald's slogan, 'I'm lovin' it', or the line in Estelle's song, 'I'm liking this American boy' – because of what seems to be our growing fondness for the continuous form.

Simple past

English's simple past tense really is simple. It has a perfectly straightforward, no-messing function: to show that the verb's action happened in the past and is finished. As for its form; just as our nouns only have to add an 's' to turn them into plurals, so the vast majority of English's verbs go into the past merely by adding an '-ed' to the end of the root form – 'Yesterday, all my troubles seemed so far away'; 'The boy kicked the ball'; 'The conman kissed the aardvark.'

The '-ed' ending applies throughout – first, second and third persons, singular and plural – so the conventional table is remarkable for its monotony.

I kissed	We kissed
You kissed	You kissed
He/she/it kissed	They kissed

The simple past can cause a few problems with spelling (verbs of two or more syllables which end in a single consonant double that consonant – 'admitted', 'preferred' – except if the first syllable is stressed, in which case the ending stays the same – 'entered' versus 'interred'), but that's not the grammar's fault or problem. There are only two footnote-worthy further points to make about the form's pronunciation: (1) that verbs ending in 't' or 'd' add '-ed' with the 'e' pronounced in an extra syllable ('batted', 'raided', 'floated'); and (2) as with the 's' plurals on nouns, our spelling conventions hide the fact that there are actually two different consonants used in that '-ed' ending – a voiced 'd' after voiced consonants and vowels, but a voiceless 't' after voiceless consonants – 'seemed' is pronounced with a 'd', 'kissed' with a 't'.

Originally, the 'ed' was pronounced as a separate syllable – 'kiss-ed' – but that began to be dropped in early Modern English, a new clipped pronunciation that proved particularly handy to dramatists working in blank verse and looking to save a precious syllable – hence, for example, Shakespeare's 'star-cross'd lovers'. Over a century later, traditionalists were still lamenting the loss of the '-ed' syllable. In 1712, Jonathan Swift was still complaining about "'drudg'd", "disturb'd", "rebuk'd", "fledg'd" and a thousand others ... where by leaving out a vowel to save a syllable, we form so jarring a sound, and so difficult to utter, that I have often wondered how it could ever obtain'.[2]

Seasoned language-learners would have heard alarms whooping in this section's second sentence, and with justification because although the vast majority of our verbs do form their past with those easy-peasy 'add "-ed"' rules, there are some irregular verbs which don't.

First, there are the faithful irregulars, 'to have', 'to do' and 'to say', whose past forms in standard English are 'had', 'did' and 'said', and 'to be', whose simple past has 'was' for I, and he/she/it and 'were' everywhere else. Again, there are lots of dialect variations; notably 'done' instead of 'did' and 'was' or 'were' throughout. Incidentally, the strange forms of the simple past for 'to be' and 'to go' are borrowings from other verbs. Old English actually had three verbs where we have only 'to be', 'beon', 'esan' and 'wesan', and 'to go' nicked its past form from the now archaic verb, 'wend'.

But there are quite a lot of other irregular verbs, which turn into the past tense not by adding '-ed' but principally by changing the vowel in the root form – 'begin/began', 'dig/dug', 'freeze/froze', 'swim/swam'. (See Appendix 2: List of irregular verbs, p. 223.)

About twenty of those irregular verbs – such as 'cut', 'put' and 'set' – don't change form at all. Which can be confusing. 'I cut the bread' could be in the present tense as a statement of ongoing policy, or it could be a past form referring to one act of bread-cutting that happened long ago.

These irregular forms are the English verbs' version of the nouns which use a different vowel sound to shift into the plural, like 'man/men'. These vowel-shifting systems for verbs and nouns

---

2   Jonathan Swift, 'A Proposal for Correcting, Improving and Ascertaining the English Tongue' (1712).

are both survivors from Old English and in fact go all the way back to Proto-Indo-European. And very probably, much, much further back than that.

Proto-Indo-European's method of forming a past tense by changing the vowel survived intact for over three thousand years, until an alternative formula, of keeping the root vowel and adding a 't' and 'd' to the end, developed in proto-Germanic, spoken by tribes in northern Germany, Jutland and southern Sweden between, roughly, 500 BC and 500 AD. These innovative 't' or 'd' endings possibly evolved from a reduced form of 'do' – something like, 'he talk-did' – and was first applied to new or loan verbs. These were difficult to put into the past with a vowel change because by that time many or most of the original rules governing the various vowel changes in Proto-Indo-European had become scrambled or lost. (Although the lingering echo of those rules can still be detected in the patterns of many of our irregulars, such as 'ring/rang' and 'bear/bore' – that second pair, for example, in Proto-Indo-European was 'bher/bhor'.)

For the same reason, there was no longer any reliable way of predicting what a verb's past form would be, so the new rule was more than welcome. By the time of Old English, only about a quarter of the verbs changed vowel for the past, with the majority keeping the same root form and taking the '-te' or '-de' ending that is the forerunner of our '-ed'. (A small number of Old English verbs were all-over-the-shop irregular – not only the stalwart irregulars 'beon', 'habban', 'don' ('do'), 'secgan' ('say'), and 'gan' ('go'), but also 'libban' ('live'), 'witan' ('know'), and about a dozen others.) All new verbs since early Old English had taken the new '-ed' ending, a practice which gained a huge boost after the Norman Conquest when the language acquired lots and lots of new words. That process continues. When Twitter inspired a new verb, nobody considered using 'twote' instead of 'tweeted'.

Replacing that ancient vowel-change system with the '-ed' ending has been a continuing part of English's simplification. Old English and Middle English had about 400 irregular verbs; modern standard English has about half that number, even with the addition of many extra irregulars with prefixes like 'missell' or 'overbid'. The regularising process has been even more effective in American English, living proof of the theory that the greater the population, the more contact with other languages and the larger the number of adult learners of a language, the simpler its grammar will be.

But this efficient streamlining of the past tense comes at a price. As Pinker points out, that 'd' or 't' ending can be difficult to hear; hence misspellings such as 'use to', 'suppose to', and indeed 'ice-cream', which started life as 'iced' – similarly 'sour cream' and 'mince meat'.[3] Another plus for irregular verbs, and another explanation for why they exist in the first place, is that they're rather pleasing to use – 'sing/sang', 'blow/blew', 'swing/swung'. Their appeal endures: British as well as American Modern English has introduced a few irregular past forms to previously regular verbs – 'knelt' and even 'caught' became established only in the late eighteenth and nineteenth centuries, and the award for most recently created irregular past goes to the still-slightly-possibly-infra-dig-and-certainly-still-Americanish 'snuck', whose first citation in the *Oxford English Dictionary* is from 1887.[4]

As always, the verbs which managed to resist the regularising process are the most common. If verbs become less common, they either become regularised or they cause native speakers just a bit of the confusion and uncertainty that is the adult learner's lot. Hence our current uses of both 'dreamed' and 'dreamt' or 'leaped' and 'leapt', where the irregular forms have reached the first stage of being replaced by regulars and we aren't quite sure which to use. The next

---

3   Pinker, *Words and Rules*, pp. 18 and 19.

4   Ibid., p. 76.

stage is replacement which is what has happened to less common verbs such as 'beseech', 'chide' and 'slay'.

Unlikely though it may sound, the regular and irregular forms of English's simple past tense have become a hotly contested ideological battleground over the last twenty-odd years, specifically in the two competing explanations of how we acquire them as children. First, they were seized on by Chomsky's supporters as evidence of the Language Acquisition Device at work. As Chomsky's most prominent follower, Pinker, has explained in *Words and Rules*, a book that is largely devoted to English's simple past verbs, it seemed that irregular forms are memorised by rote but the regular forms of the past tense are generated by a grammatical rule (add '-ed' to the end of the verb).

By this analysis, when we're about to use a simple past tense, we first consult our mental dictionaries and either retrieve the stored irregular form or, if there's no form to be retrieved, default to the application of the regular rule, which would have to have been generated by the rule-seeking innate grammar-parser of our Language Acquisition Device. What particularly excited Chomskyites like Pinker is the manner in which English-speaking toddlers learn the simple past forms in identifiable stages: one, sporadic use of the irregular forms of our most common verbs; two, intermittent use of '-ed' endings on some regulars; and then, crucially, the mistaken application of the add '-ed' rule to both regulars and irregulars, so that young kids produce incorrect forms like 'goed', 'cutted' and 'breaked' as they bash away at the language like they bang away at the computer keyboard and overclick the mouse; then, four, sorting the two sorts of verb out and getting the forms right.

Chomskyites have taken this U-shaped development to be clinching proof of the workings of our innate grammatical facility, of the Language Acquisition Device seeking out a rule and applying it over-zealously. However, this has since come under vigorous attack from those who favour a non-innate, connectionist explanation. Their very persuasive case points to the increasingly successful attempts to create computer models that broadly mimic how neuroscientists think neural networks function: these have generated irregular and regular forms with uncannily similar U-shaped development as English-speaking children, and with the same pattern of errors. There's no need for some innate rule-search-and-apply device to explain the peculiar pattern of our irregular-versus-regular verb acquisition; the experience of exposure to the language is enough.[5]

The simple past is also where non-standard speakers are often thought to be making mistakes, when their dialect has a different form – 'done' instead of standard's 'did', for example, or 'seen' instead of 'saw'.

As we will see, the simple-past forms also turn up in a few places other than the simple past. In 1924 the grammarian Otto Jespersen – he was Danish, incidentally, which explains the penultimate example – outlined four additional uses of the form apart from its function as a simple past, although I'm not sure the fourth still applies.

> Unreality in present tense (if we *knew*; I wish I *knew*)
> Future time (it is time you *went* to bed)
> Shifted present tense (how did you know I *was* a Dane?)
> All times (men *were* deceivers ever)[6]

---

5 Pinker, *Words and Rules*. The connectionist explanation is given in Elman et al., *Rethinking Innateness: A Connectionist Perspective on Development*, pp. 130ff.

6 Otto Jespersen, *The Philosophy of Grammar* (London: George Allen & Unwin, 1924), p. 56.

Past continuous

We form this tense by using a past form of 'to be' as an auxiliary, placing that before the stem of the verb and adding an '-ing' to the end: 'The boy was kicking the ball'; 'It was raining.'

A look at the past continuous might make the tense–aspect distinction a little clearer and less like something worth crossing the street to avoid. This is a past construction, like the simple past, describing an event that's definitely in the past, over and done with, been and gone, but adding a continuous aspect: it's an event that carried on for some time before it came to an end. And it is a continuous aspect – not habitual, when we would use 'used to' – so this is a tense that specifies a certain sort of action – begun in the past, went on continuously, not just every now and again but definitely all the time, then finished.

The past continuous usually turns up with a simple past verb when there's a sense of interruption or at least intersection – 'They were ambling along the High Street when one of them spontaneously combusted'; 'I was making the milkman a cup of tea when all my clothes just seemed to fall off.'

Take the example of our young footballer. 'The boy was kicking the ball': that isn't something that we'd usually say on its own; it seems to cry out for something else, a bit of context, another event. So, 'The boy was kicking the ball . . . um, with his friend . . .' or '. . . against a wall' (because either this goes with a when-something-happened construction to describe the something that would have to happen at the very moment he was kicking the ball, or the kicking's got to happen all the time, so the ball's got to come back to him each time) . . . and still the natural option seems to go with a 'when' + simple past, though now with a greatly expanded interruptible time frame, no longer the moment of boot-to-ball kicking impact but the entire ball-kicking episode.

However, on a much less fussy note, we also use the past continuous when something is being interpreted – 'Julia told Jim she loved him but she was leading him a merry dance' – and when we tell stories, to distinguish between scene-setting, which gets the past continuous, and actions, which receive the simple past – 'The sun was shining, the birds were singing and the boy was kicking his ball. Suddenly, an alien spaceship landed on the pitch.' We also use the past continuous in casual conversation, as a marker of informality and sometimes of politeness or tentativeness.

'So I was wondering if you'd like to come out on a date?'
'I was hoping you'd ask me that. Were you planning anything in particular?'
'You free tonight?'
'Yes, I am, actually.'
'Great. I've got two tickets for the Millwall-Brentford game.'
'Right . . . I was thinking more of a Nando's?'

Present perfect

We form this tense by using 'has' or 'have' as an auxiliary followed by the past participle of the main verb. With regular verbs, that past participle has the same '-ed' tagged to the end as the simple past form. Irregular verbs take their own idiosyncratic form of the past participle – 'sung', 'put', 'known', 'forgotten' and all the others in that third column on pages 223–31. So – 'I have walked', 'You have talked', 'He has stalked', 'We have seen the light' and 'They have kept the faith.'

I have always been against it.	We have brought our own sandwiches.
You have just fallen into the lava.	You lot have turned up early.
He has bought an ostrich on eBay.	They have completely ruined the coastline.

The form may be straightforward enough, but English's present perfect is a tense that causes real problems, for many of us native speakers, if we use non-standard versions of the irregular past participle – more of that anon. It also bewilders all EFL students. Each and every single one of them.

Why their misery? It's not the form but the function of the present perfect that confounds adult learners of our language, because it's a really complicated tense, though not to us natives who use it with unthinking grace.

Basically, the present perfect marks the verb with a past tense but one that has some sort of relevance to the present. As EFL students struggle to understand, but as you know without knowing it, the present perfect is used in three different contexts: (1) when we talk about an action that started in the past and continues into the present ('I have waited ten minutes and a bus still hasn't come'); (2) when an action has finished but very recently ('I have just sat down on a ripe tomato'); and (3) when an action is finished but – and if you're a bit confused by this explanation, spare a thought for non-native speakers faced with this – that action is placed within an overarching time scheme that continues into the present. For example, 'I have seen an eclipse once in the last twenty years' or 'He has been to prison': in both cases the action is finished – the eclipse witnessed, the prison sentence served – but the context, of the last twenty years and the overall life, continues.

The present perfect has to be non-committally vague about the timing of the event because as soon as the time is specified and the event stated to be past then the simple past has to be used – 'I saw an eclipse when I was a kid'; 'Last year he did six months in Pentonville.'

At least, that's the textbook rule. But our use of the present perfect can be a bit laxer than that. Take the example given in the *Oxford Modern English Grammar*: 'The linesman's given the decision but what astounds me is that he has sent Taricco off before he spoke to the linesman.' According to the manuals, the present perfect's 'has given' and 'has sent' should be simple pasts because of the specific past-time reference at the end – 'before he spoke to the linesman.' However, the present perfect is actually the favoured tense of football pundits. So much so that one linguist has labelled it 'the footballer's present perfect'.[7] My own impression is that it's conspicuous on programmes like *Match of the Day* but has a much more widespread usage, as a story-telling tense along with the simple present, used to give past, completed actions relevance and immediacy – 'So I've said to him, don't you dare. But he has gone and done it anyway – he has kicked that ball and it has headed straight for that window and he has smashed it into smithereens.'

One of the reasons the present perfect is noticeable on *Match of the Day* is that it is used by ex-footballers, so this is one of those not so common occasions when working-class people who have left school at sixteen and who haven't made any attempt to standardise their grammar are invited to express their opinions as experts, and in doing so happily employ non-standard present perfect forms. 'He's went into the box, he's took a dive and the ref's gave a penalty.'

(Non-standard present perfects crop up quite regularly in the back pages of the local newspaper in my home town, Kirkcaldy, where the football reporter uses working-class Scottish past

---

7 Jim Walker, 'The Strange Phenomenon of the Footballer's Perfect', in Genevieve Girard-Gillet, ed., *Étrange/Étranger: études de linguistique anglaise* (Publications de Université de Saint-Étienne, 2008), pp. 21–32.

participles without having them corrected, as they would be by subeditors on a larger organ – 'The lights may have went out at Balmoor Stadium on Saturday but Raith Rovers found that missing spark . . .'; 'Raith Rovers have more than rode their luck at times recently'; 'David Smith's loan deal from Hearts has ran out.')[8]

Although non-standard's past participles often stand out, the process of dialect levelling has had a devastating effect on the many weird and wonderful forms found in non-standard English in the olden days. For example, instead of standard's regular past participle 'climbed', 'clom' appeared in some Scottish and northern English dialects and 'clombed' in northeast Scotland and Somerset; where standard had 'written', dialects in Edinburgh, Warwickshire and Somerset had 'rote', 'thunk' turned up as the past participle of 'think' in Yorkshire, 'wentn' as the past of 'go' in Northumberland, and 'squeezed' was irregularised in Lincolnshire as 'skwoznd'.

Most of the non-standard past participles listed on page after page by Joseph Wright in 1905 have disappeared by now. In place of regional exotica, non-standard dialects have been converging to share many forms, like 'went' instead of standard's 'gone' and 'ran' instead of 'run', though still maintaining many differences from standard's past participles, particularly with verbs like 'go' and 'break' where standard has three forms, which non-standard reduces to two.

Non-standard dialects can also have a different auxiliary verb from standard. Apparently, in some dialects of the east Midlands and west East Anglia, the auxiliary 'to be' can still be heard in the present perfect – 'I'm been there; I'm seen him.'[9] This preserves an earlier

8 *Fife Free Press*, 3 February 2006, 1 November 2007 and 31 January 2013. Grateful thanks to my father for spotting these. An example of a non-standard Scottish irregular past participle evading the subs on a bigger paper comes from the *Guardian*'s back pages of 22 August 2012, when Ronnie Esplin reported on Celtic's game against Helsingborg, 'Neil Lennon's side might have rode their luck at times'.

9 David Britain, 'Grammatical Variation in England', in *Language in the British Isles*, ed. David Britain (Cambridge University Press, 2007).

formation of the tense which was still popular in Shakespeare's time, when 'to be' was often used as the auxiliary in the present perfect.

That kind of variant auxiliary might seem quaint and sweet, but a far more popular variant is less gently dealt with, namely the negatives, where instead of 'has not' and 'have not', many dialects on both sides of the Atlantic have 'ain't'. (Again, I think it's worth pointing out that this isn't a mistaken or inadequate form – neither Bachman nor Turner or indeed Overdrive got anything wrong when they sang 'you ain't seen nothin yet'.) This is one of five occasions when 'ain't' turns up in negative constructions – where standard has 'has not', 'have not', 'am not', 'is not' and 'are not' – but no matter what its meaning or function, 'ain't' is, for many, just beyond the pale. In the eighteenth and nineteenth centuries, 'ain't' was a form used by some members of the aristocracy, but it was also a feature of Cockney, which amateur language guardians have always held in particular revulsion because it's an urban dialect with no quaintly rural connotations and because it's the non-standard dialect that's the nearest to standard, so when it does differ from standard, the variations are lampooned and lambasted. Its reputation is so bad that in *Usage and Abusage*, Eric Partridge had to stay strong as he forced himself to deal with 'ain't': 'an error so illiterate that I blush to record it'.

Finally, two less noticed variations. For some reason, the present perfect is particularly popular in Scotland, so that Scottish children acquire it earlier than other British kids, who in turn are quicker to pick up the present perfect than American children, who are four or five years old by the time they've got to grips with a form which isn't used quite so much as in Britain.[10] A second peculiarity comes from Ireland where, presumably under the influence of Irish, the tense often takes the form of 'to be' + 'after' + '-ing' – so standard's 'I have eaten' becomes 'I am after eating'. Perhaps propelled by anxiety about

---

10   V. C. Gathercole, 'The Acquisition of the Present Perfect', *Journal of Child Language* 13(3) (1986), pp. 537–60.

the correctness of the form, the present perfect is less used in Irish English – apart from some Irish English-speakers whose hyper-correction leads them to overuse the form instead of the simple past in sentences like 'He's broken the window yesterday.'[11]

Present perfect continuous

This is formed with the auxiliary verbs 'has/have been' + the '-ing' form of the main verb – 'He has been drinking heavily'; 'Have you been following *Big Brother*?'

This tense is often used instead of the simple present perfect. Not too shockingly, the present perfect continuous is usually applied for continuous actions ('I have been waiting for a bus for ten minutes' would actually come more naturally to us than 'I have waited'). However, there can be distinct nuances between the two forms. 'I have been watching *Dr Who*' definitely places that action as either continuing or recently finished, whereas 'I have watched *Dr Who*' just doesn't. 'I've cleaned the oven' places that action as completed, a chore ticked off the list, whereas 'I've been cleaning the oven' would normally indicate that the work is still ongoing. The continuous form also conveys that an event was repeated – 'I've been going there, man and boy, since the 1970s' versus 'I have gone there a few times'.

As with other continuous constructions, 'state' verbs like 'know', 'believe' and 'like' don't usually appear in the present perfect continuous, although the tense is possible with wishes and desires – 'Ever since she upped and left, Jim has been wanting Julia back.'

---

11   John Harris, 'The Grammar of Irish English', in *Real English*, ed. James Milroy and Lesley Milroy (Longman, 1993).

Past perfect

We form this tense with the auxiliary verb 'had' + the past participle of the main verb – 'I had bought the tickets for the three of us but after ten minutes he had walked out and she had just disappeared.'

The past perfect often turns up with time-placing words like 'after' or 'before' or 'when', because its main use is to place one action further back in the past than another – 'I had just been to the Falklands before I went to Buenos Aires, so there was a bit of a problem with my visa'; 'He had never broken a window until he kicked that ball straight at it'; 'We had barely finished breakfast when the ceiling fell in.'

The auxiliary 'had' is the same for all persons, singular and plural. Nor does it vary much within different dialects. However, as with the present perfect, non-standard past participles often vary from standard's. And when they are noticed, the attention is rarely favourable.

Past perfect continuous

This is formed by the past perfect of 'to be' ('had been' throughout) – together with the '-ing' participle of the main verb – 'I had been sleeping'; 'You had been trying to call me'; 'It had been raining all day'. With an auxiliary that doesn't change much within non-standard dialects and a straightforward '-ing' form of the verb, this is a tense which shows probably the least variation in non-standard English from the standard dialect.

This being a continuous construction, it is most readily applied to repeated or continued actions – 'She had been running for half an hour when the sun finally appeared'; 'He had been drinking far too much coffee before I started him on herbal teas'; 'Jim had been crying about Julia all night.' Sometimes the continuous event can continue beyond the specified time – 'She had been dating him for several years before she discovered he was really into line-dancing'

– possibly this discovery ended the relationship, which would make it a conventional past perfect continuous, placed further back in the past before another past verb ('discovered'); but then again, the construction leaves it open for that continuous dating process to keep going, beyond the discovery and feasibly up to the present.

Simple future

Interestingly, although English-speaking children seem to have no problem in thinking about the future, they do tend to find it more difficult to master future constructions than past ones.[12] Presumably, this is because our past tenses are encoded by the main verbs whereas English's futures rely on auxiliaries to do the work. Hence, too, the technical explanation that English doesn't really have a future tense.

Another reason for young children's difficulties could be that English has a variety of ways of expressing the future.

The basic method is to use 'will' as an auxiliary together with the stem of the main verb. 'Shall' is also used as an auxiliary, in standard English, though rarely in non-standard, and traditionalists still like to maintain the old division, that 'shall' goes with 'I' and 'we', and 'will' with the second and third persons, and that any deviation from this is either incorrect or correctly signals greater emphasis – 'You shall go to the ball.' Actually, like 'one' as a pronoun, 'shall' is increasingly unpopular, too posh by half and no longer a feasible option for most standard speakers, and now survives mostly in first-person questions or suggestions ('Shall I call a cab?' 'Shall we?').

Having said that, many EFL manuals now teach that the principal form of the English future is now the root form of the verb

---

12   Tomasello, *Constructing a Language*, p. 221.

following 'to be going to'. In the normal course of events, this phrase would be eroded to become a new auxiliary, 'gonna' – which has more or less happened in speech, but definitely not in writing, where the full form is retained and, such is the conservatism that comes with literacy, where it will remain in its full form for a long, long time to come.

But English also drafts in other tenses to talk about the future. There's the simple present, which is often used with specifically timed actions – 'The play starts at eight'; 'We ride at dawn.' The present continuous can also come in handy in similar situations – 'The play's starting in five minutes' – particularly if there is some sort of arrangement involved – 'He's arriving on Thursday, so she's taking the day off.' Less frequently, we can also use 'to be' + infinitive – 'I am to go to Bratislava on Monday for a conference' – if we want to convey a sense of definiteness and obligation.

A construction that baffles many EFL students is our use of the simple present for the future after time words, like 'when', 'after', 'until' or 'before' – 'I'll give it to you when I meet you next week'; 'As soon as he sees the state of that window, he's going to go ballistic.' 'When I will meet you . . .', 'As soon as he will see . . .' – they are very common errors among adult learners. Quite understandably so, but they're still errors, and ones which we would never make, at least while sober.

Future continuous

Unacknowledged by many grammars, English now has two constructions for the future continuous – 'will be' + '-ing' form of the main verb, and 'to be going to' + verb with '-ing': 'I'll be seeing you'; 'They're going to be repairing the window tomorrow.'

The various forms of the future can carry subtle nuances of meaning. The future continuous often comes in handy because it's neutral, referring to future events as happening as a matter of course, as in the promise/threat of the Police song, 'I'll be watching you.' Compare the other available forms – 'I'm going to be watching you' – that's stronger, expressing a firmer intention or prediction; 'I'll watch you' – also with added intention; 'I'm to watch you' – there's the obligation involved of a given assignment.

The future continuous crops up a lot in our questions, where its neutrality and possibly its longer form help make queries polite or gentle. Compare 'Will you be eating with us tonight?' and 'Are you going to be eating with us tonight?' with 'Will you eat with us tonight?', which is either a less tentative question or a definite invitation.

Future perfect

A marvellously Utopian label for a tense that is also blessed with the gift of time travel.

Our future perfects are formed by 'will' (or 'to be going to') + 'have' + past participle – 'I will have left by tomorrow morning'; 'By the time she's finished, she's going to have eaten porridge out of all three bowls, she'll have wrecked a chair and slept in all the beds'; 'The glazier cancelled so now the window will not have been repaired by the end of next week.' In each example, the action is viewed from a point in the future when it will have already happened.

Future perfect continuous

This bears the same relationship to the future perfect that the present perfect continuous has with the present perfect – i.e., if we're doing the time-travel business of going into the future and looking back on a still-future action as past but the action was continuous. We use this tense mostly with sentences describing how long the action or event lasted, so it usually appears with expressions that start with 'for', whereas the future perfect tends to appear with 'by'.

The tense is formed by putting together 'will/to be going to' + 'have been' + '- ing' form of the main verb – 'Next week, we'll have been going out together for six months'; 'That little swine will have been kicking that ball of his for six hours straight by teatime.'

Once again, most state verbs don't work in this continuous form – 'She'll have known him for all of six months by the time they get married' is okay but 'she'll have been knowing' isn't. Similarly, the verb 'to be' doesn't really turn up either in this tense – 'I will have been being . . .' – or the future continuous –'I will be being . . .' Also, the future perfect continuous stops being available as an option as soon as an action is specified in some way, especially by time, in which case we have to use the future perfect – 'that means he's going to have appeared three times on that same chat show'; 'so that by the end of the year, I will have eaten 365 Twixes'.

Conditional

There are two tenses in the conditional: the present, formed by 'would' or 'should' + the root form of the verb; and the perfect, formed by 'would' or 'should' plus 'have' plus the past participle.

Conditional constructions usually come in two sections: the main statement and an 'if'-phrase that sets out some sort of proviso or qualification – 'If you go, I'll go'; 'I wouldn't if I were you'; 'If he hadn't kicked that damned ball, the kitchen would still have had a window.'

There are three principal types of conditional construction in English, none of them easy for adult learners, or indeed particularly easy for English-speaking children (by four years old, many children try out conditional constructions but often don't quite get the tenses right – 'If she didn't leave the rabbit's hutch open, the rabbit wouldn't run away'.[13]

Type 1: both sections refer to a future event, but although the verb in the main statement takes a future tense, the conditional 'if'-section stays in the present – 'I'll go ballistic if he breaks that window'; 'You're going to be sick if you eat any more of those Twixes – they're supposed to last a whole year.' At its core, this construction conveys an 'if X then Y' predictive certainty. However, we also use it to give permission ('Yes, you can stay up late if you tidy your room'), to put forward a possibility ('If it gets any hotter, I may have to change into my itsy-bitsy teeny-weeny yellow polka-dot bikini') or to dole out advice ('If you're going to Skegness, you should visit all the many attractions'). Sometimes, we use 'should' in the 'if'-phrase to veer away from certainty and towards possibility – 'If you should go to Skegness . . .' 'Should' can sometimes also replace 'if' – 'Should you ever find yourself in Skegness . . .'

Type 2: this moves the conditional from prediction to speculation, because these constructions refer to theoretical realities. It's one of the unacknowledged tics of British English to use this conditional a lot in requests, where other languages and American English have normal, blunter constructions. 'Could we have the house red, please?' 'I was wondering if I could possibly try this in the large?' The first time I heard an American ask for something, I was outraged – a young chap in a pub who walked up to the bar and informed the barman, 'I need a beer.' The barman looked at him as though he had just shape-shifted into a fully clothed rhinoceros. Oblivious, the American continued: 'Gimme a pint of lager.'

To form type 2 conditionals, we put the verb in the 'if'-section in the past and the verb in the main section into the conditional,

---

13 Both insight and example come from Eve V. Clark, *First Language Acquisition* (2nd edn, Cambridge University Press, 2009), p. 251.

normally using the auxiliaries 'would' or 'should' – 'If I ruled the world, every day would be the first day of spring'; 'If he knew about her shenanigans, he would leave her on the spot'; 'If I ever saw a ghost, I'd scream and scream until I was sick.'

The past tenses in those examples aren't past – they're unreal. And when language deals with the unreal, verbs can change, and as in many Indo-European languages, what they can change into are the distinctive forms of the subjunctive.

Ah, the subjunctive. It's surely up there with 'gerund' as one of the most unenticing of all grammar's many unenticing terms; and understandably so given that some languages go in for them in a big way, suddenly presenting their learners with a whole new raft of verb endings to tackle unreal or wished-for events. In English, though, the subjunctive doesn't really exist as a separate entity. Most of us have dispensed with it as a working form. Even for those who keep it as an option, the subjunctive is nigh-on invisible, because it can appear on only a few, specific occasions.

In the present tense, the subjunctive takes the bare infinitive form throughout, so is only noticed in the third-person singular when it doesn't take an '-s'. Very few of us still use the present subjunctive in everyday speech ('I suggested that she go to Skegness with me'), but it turns up in various fossilised phrases, usually expressing a wish – 'God bless you', 'God save the Queen'. The Lord's Prayer preserves a list of subjunctively formed wishes – 'thy kingdom come', 'thy will be done' – but the strangeness of the constructions to modern ears explains why, when an RE teacher got us high-school third-years to translate the Lord's Prayer into contemporary English, everyone in my class put 'you shall be done'. Part of the problem there, of course, was 'be' – the subjunctive form of the present tense throughout, as in 'God be with you'. That subjunctive 'be' still appears, though almost never in everyday conversation and almost always in very formal, often legal, contexts – 'if the shipment be delayed' and 'if he be found culpable for the damage'.

There's also a past subjunctive, which takes the same form as the simple past. It only exists as an identifiably separate construction with the verb 'to be', which declines with 'were' throughout. Hence 'If I were a rich man'; 'If she were to move to Bristol'; 'If he were ever to break a window, I'd make him pay for it'. Many grammars insist on a 'were' instead of a 'was' in such structures, but that is to ignore the fact that a 'was' is often possible but with a slight difference in meaning, bringing the verb towards the realm of the possible rather than keeping it strictly subjunctively theoretical – 'If a huge asteroid were to obliterate life on Earth' versus 'If that little gobshite was to break the window, I swear I'd swing for him.'

Type 3: to form the third conditional, we put the verb in the 'if'-section into the past perfect and the verb in the main section into the perfect conditional, formed by 'would' or 'should' plus 'have' plus the past participle.

This is the tense of recrimination and reproach, regret and remorse, of things that weren't done but should have been done, of how things might have been if they'd turned out differently. 'If I'd known you were coming, I'd have baked a cake'; 'If I had known you were baking a cake, I wouldn't have eaten all of those Twixes'; 'If he hadn't kicked that ball so hard, he wouldn't have broken the window.' Sometimes, we can try a slightly different construction by replacing the 'if' with a 'had' and then inverting the word order – 'Had I known you were baking a cake . . .'

Their fairly complicated nature and the grammatical illiteracy that has come from nobody ever, ever teaching this subject, explains why some of us get a bit lost with type 3 sentences, as evidenced by the frequent mistake, which can often be heard in speech as well as seen in print, of putting an 'of' instead of the 'have' in the perfect conditional – 'I should of done it'; 'I might of known it'.

I've used 'would' and 'should' for most of those conditional constructions but there are other 'modal' verbs which can also fit into many of them: 'can/could', 'may/might', 'must', 'have to/had to', and 'ought'. They all express an attitude about a statement – implying that there's an obligation involved or that the action is possible or certain or necessary or permitted. They are distinctive in having no continuous form and, in standard English, for having no final '-s' in the third-person singular. And 'must' and 'ought' exist only in the present tense, so have to be replaced by, respectively, a form of ' have to' or a 'shall' or 'should'. Excepting Scottish dialects of English which have the ability to use 'double modals' – 'I'll can do it tomorrow', 'He might can do it.' (Scottish dialects are also distinguished by not having 'may' and 'ought' as well as the more commonly deleted 'shall'.)

There are also three tricky little semi-modals: 'need', 'dare' and 'used to'. 'Need' and 'dare' can also be ordinary verbs, of course, but when they are applied semi-modally, they can take on the modal habit of maintaining the same root form throughout and are followed by the bare, infinitive form – so 'He needs a kick up the arse' but 'He need not worry.' An additional little twist is that they can also be used semi-modally with auxiliaries, in which case they behave normally – 'He doesn't need to worry'; 'They wouldn't dare to try.' 'Used to' is a favoured construction for us, often replacing simple past tenses for actions that were frequent or continuous – 'I used to love her, but it's all over now'; 'I knew the bride when she used to rock and roll.' All well and good, but trouble looms large when we – not just EFL learners but us native speakers – try to turn 'used to' into a negative or a question. The 'correct' form stipulated by the manuals is to drop the 'd' in both – 'I didn't use to . . .'; 'Did you use to?' – although some traditional grammars still claim that the negative form should follow the usual auxiliary pattern – 'I used not to . . .' and even 'I usedn't to . . .', which to my ears sound much less preferable.

As well as those modals, English has three verbs which work both normally and as auxiliary verbs: 'be', 'have' and 'do'. 'Be' is drafted in for the continuous forms, 'have' for the perfect forms and 'do' for the simple tenses when they need an auxiliary verb to make questions and negatives.

Questions first. Human languages have discovered various ways to ask questions. Russian, like Latin and many African languages, uses a question word; in Spanish, the construction remains exactly the same as a statement and relies on intonation to signal that it has changed into a query.

English has four ways of forming a question.

(1) reverse the order of subject and verb. This was once possible for all verbs and was the principal method of forming a question, but now it applies only to the verb 'to be' – 'Is he okay?'; 'Are you sure?'; 'Were they upset?'

(2) with verbs that have auxiliaries, reverse the order of the first auxiliary and the subject – 'Can we fix it?'; 'Will he be going?'; 'Could I care less?'

(3) add a question word to the start of the sentence and reverse the subject–verb order – 'When can you make it?'; 'Why are you upset?'; 'What will you say?' The question word can also be a subject, in which case there is no change in the word order, as in 'Who killed Cock Robin?'

(4) excepting 'to be', with verbs in the simple present and simple past, which have no auxiliaries, we import 'do' as a 'dummy' at the start of the question, keep the regular word order and change the verb into its bare infinitive form – 'Does he take sugar?'; 'Do you want to dance?'; 'Did she cheat on Jim?'; 'Did you really eat all those Twixes?'

'Do' began to turn up as an auxiliary in the fifteenth century, when it was used mainly as an extra tense marker in the simple present and simple past – 'I do go'; 'He did go'. It seems to have been an 'empty', meaning-free option, at least according to one proto-linguist in 1530: 'I do is a verbe moche comenly used in our tonge to be put before other verbes: as it is all one to say, "I do speke . . ." and "I speke"'.[14] This usage declined in standard English in the latter half of the sixteenth century, although it was retained in some dialects. Nowadays, 'do' turns up to mark habitual actions in rural (i.e., rapidly vanishing) dialects in the southwest of England – 'I do go into town every day.' A preverbal 'do' is also used in some US dialects in the Deep South and in, to use its linguistic label, African American Vernacular English, where 'done' before a simple past has the force of 'already'. This auxiliary 'done' appears in one British English dialect, although it's not one commonly heard, seeing as how it's the often curious variety spoken by the several hundred inhabitants of Tristan da Cunha, the British colony on a volcano in the middle of the Atlantic, halfway between South Africa and South America.

Like the other Germanic languages, English used to rely on subject–verb word order swap to turn simple tenses into questions, but the dummy 'do' began to appear as an option in the fifteenth century. By 1600, both constructions were equally available to Shakespeare. 'Know you any?' Claudio asks Hero in the marriage scene in Act 4 Scene 1 of *Much Ado About Nothing*. 'Do you see yonder cloud that's almost in shape of a camel?' Hamlet asks Polonius (Act 3 Scene 2), not 'See you . . .' The dummy 'do' construction seems to be the one he preferred. 'What do you read, my lord?' Polonius asks Hamlet, using the simple present where we would use the continuous, because the present continuous had yet to be developed. The two constructions continued to be used for some time thereafter. In *The Mill on the Floss*, published in 1860, though set some thirty or forty years before,

---

14 John Palsgrave, *L'éclaircissement de la langue française* (1530), cited in Traugott, *History of English Syntax*, p. 138.

George Eliot gives Maggie Tulliver an old reversed word order structure for a question immediately followed by another question with a dummy 'do' – 'How came you to be walking here? Did you come to meet me?'

'Do' was also conscripted into service in negative statements. Old English once had the straightforward 'ne' before verbs, in all tenses, as did Middle English, which first added a 'nat' or a 'not' to accompany the 'ne' and then dropped the 'ne', so that the predominant form 'not' could precede verbs – 'It not belongs to you' in *Henry IV Part 2* (Act 4 Scene 1) – or come after them – 'I know not your cousin', or, obeying the then rule against pronouns arriving last in negative statements, 'I know him not'. The traditionalists' bugbear of double negatives actually has a long and distinguished history, going back to Anglo-Saxon days and still more than usable by Shakespeare – a couple of scenes after the 'not belongs to you', Falstaff scoffs, 'There's never none of these demure boys come to any proof' (*Henry IV Part 2*, Act 4 Scene 3).

'Do' is also now roped in to fill in for the missing auxiliary in simple tenses when we form tag questions. These are the little questions we shove on to the end of statements to elicit agreement – 'He is daft, isn't he?'; 'I have done it, haven't I?'; 'We should go, shouldn't we?' We native speakers do this a lot, in all dialects. (One of the tics that French people notice when English speakers speak French is the wild overuse of their catch-all question tag, 'n'est-ce pas?')

The rules for the formulation of these tags are specific and quite complex, involving word order reversal, the swapping of negatives and positives so that negative questions follow positive statements and positive questions come after negatives, and, except for the verb 'to be', which just reverses ('He is, isn't he')[15] the use of 'do' as the

---

15 The one exception to this exception is the first-person singular which takes a third-person tag – 'I am, aren't I?' I remember this completely foxing me when I was a child and kept trying 'amn't I?' but knew that it was somehow not right.

missing auxiliary in tags appended to simple tenses – 'We saw him, didn't we?'; 'You really like him, don't you?'

Working-class Scottish English often has a much simpler tag system – 'Eh?' (pronounced like the first capital letter in the alphabet) or 'Eh no?' One of the interesting and much noticed developments in many non-standard dialects – especially in urban areas in the south of England – has been the widespread adoption of another much simpler tag question system, one that was developed by various immigrant groups. Instead of all those different pronouns and reversed auxiliaries, this system uses just one form – 'innit?' This was already the formula in some southern-English dialects for 'isn't it?' but the universal application of 'innit?', or its cherishable offspring, 'isn't it?', makes it stand out after statements that don't have an 'it is' construction – 'We should go, innit?'; 'They're having a laugh, isn't it?'; 'You just bought an ostrich on eBay, innit?' It has elegance, ease and simplicity on its side, even simpler than French's similar 'n'est-ce pas', and it seems to me to be a hugely appealing construction, but 'innit?' has been predictably lambasted as a sign of the decline of our once noble language/moral standards/western civilisation. Why the hostility? Because it's a new form introduced by people who are non-white, working class and young. No other reason. It's a prime example of a supposedly linguistic judgement being based entirely, *entirely*, on social prejudice.

Passive

Passive forms happen when the subject of an active verb becomes the 'agent', usually followed by a 'by' phrase. So the conventional, active verb in 'A maniac is running this country' becomes 'this country is being run by a maniac'.

Our passive constructions are every bit as rule-governed as question tags, with the difference that whereas EFL students can happily bypass tags as a quirk of the language reserved for just us natives, they really have to knuckle down to learn the various regulations governing our passive tenses, involving variously tensed forms of 'to be' as auxiliaries and the past participle of the verb.

Tense	Active	Passive
Simple present	takes	is taken
Present continuous	is taking	is being taken
Simple past	took	was taken
Past continuous	was taking	was being taken
Present perfect	has taken	has been taken
Past perfect	had taken	had been taken
Future	will take	will be taken
Future perfect	will have taken	will have been taken
Conditional	would take	would be taken
Perfect conditional	would have taken	would have been taken
Infinitive	to take	to be taken
Perfect infinitive	to have taken	to have been taken
Present participle/gerund	taking	being taken
Perfect participle	having taken	having been taken

Several continuous tenses are missing from that table because they don't normally exist in the passive. 'They had been taking her' or 'they would have been taking her' can't really be swapped around to start with a 'She'.

Much maligned because it's a fairly new form, but increasingly popular, 'get' is often used instead of 'be' to form passives – 'We got taken to the circus by Auntie Griselda'; 'The window got broken'; 'You will get laughed at if you wear those red corduroy trousers.' They are often interchangeable but sometimes the 'get' and 'be' constructions carry slightly different connotations. In a sentence like 'They got caught in the rain', the 'got' carries an extra implication that this was an unlooked-for and unwelcome surprise. Conversely, 'got' constructions can convey a sense of completion or achievement after struggle – 'She got selected for the British Antarctic Survey'; 'They got accepted for membership.'

The passive comes in very useful as a disinterested, objective tense ('The accused was seen proceeding swiftly in a westerly direction'; '500 ml of saline solution was added') and of course as a way of deflecting blame – a memorable example being Ronald Reagan's admissionless admission about the Iran–Contra scandal, 'Mistakes were made'.

Infinitives

Infinitives in English are formed, with all verbs, by putting 'to' before the stem – 'to go', 'to have', 'to be', 'to do', dobedobedo. Some Scottish and Geordie dialects retain an additional word with 'for to'. Unnoticed by most of us, our infinitives appear in quite a few different forms:

Present	to say
Present continuous	to be saying
Perfect	to have said
Perfect continuous	to have been saying
Passive present	to be said
Passive perfect	to have been said

In their various guises, our infinitives do a powerful job of work. They can follow some adjectives ('I am sorry to say'), they can express purpose ('He meant to say'), they can follow 'to be' verbs in plans or instructions ('Passengers are to proceed to Gate 12 for immediate boarding'), they can form the subject of a sentence ('To err is human'), they can come after certain abstract nouns, such as

VERBS

'anxiety', 'demand', 'desire', 'offer', 'refusal', 'request' and 'wish' ('It was his burning desire to eat another Twix'), they can connect two parts of a sentence ('He was distraught to hear about Julia'), they can sometimes act as alternatives to relative-clause constructions ('Do you have anything to say for yourself?' instead of 'Do you have anything that you want to say for yourself?'), and they can follow some verbs ('She dared me to eat another Twix').

Ignoring all of these functions, traditional grammars latch on to the infinitive only to warn against splitting them with a 'not' or an adverb. Well, possibly rather predictably by now, I'm going to say that this was the invention of anxious grammarians and has no relevance to any English dialect. Of course it's okay to split infinitives, as shown in the most famous split infinitive of them all: how would traditionalist grammar fiends rewrite the voiceover that introduced *Star Trek* – 'To go boldly'? 'Boldly to go'? 'To boldly go' sounds much the most natural.

When the *Star Trek* scriptwriters rejigged the intro for the second series, they were under real pressure to unsplit what had quickly become the most infamous split infinitive in the language. 'To boldly go' was said to be lazy, corrupt, the devil's work, just plain wrong. In the end, the scriptwriters held firm. *Star Trek: The Next Generation* starts with Patrick Stewart's Jean-Luc Picard repeating the mission statement of William Shatner's James T. Kirk, culminating in an infinitive which remains defiantly, proudly, unashamedly, split. (The one change that was made was the replacement of the sexist 'no man' in the original speech with a non-gender-specific alternative – 'To boldly go where no one has gone before.')

By giving it the full RSC delivery, Patrick Stewart actually pointed up the 'to boldly go' and made it sound not only acceptable but preferable; English grammar is actually quite happy to split infinitives, particularly in emphatic contexts as in its *Star Trek* appearance. Often the word that comes between the 'to' and the verb will be a negative – 'He tried to not notice'; 'She wanted to never go there again'. Sometimes adverbs can come between the 'to' and the verb, especially when the adverb is an emphasising one like 'really' or 'entirely' – 'this time I want you to really give it everything'. So 'to boldly go' is, linguistically speaking, fine.

However, it's one of those grammatical myths that split infinitives are wrong; or, more accurately, wrongly thought to be wrong but widely and unassailably so.

Actually, for much of English's life, native speakers do seem to have avoided split infinitives. Shakespeare, who manipulated the grammar of English every which way he possibly could, split an infinitive just once, and doing so to force a rhyme:

> Be it lawful I love thee as thou lov'st those
> Whom thine eyes woo as mine importune thee.
> Root pity in thy heart, that when it grows,
> Thy pity may deserve to pitied be.

(Sonnet 142)

There are several other much-cited examples of split infinitives from the seventeenth century – there are a few in the poems of John Donne and a couple appear in Pepys's diaries – but those are the examples that are always cited in a very short list and remain notable exceptions to a no-split-infinitives rule.

Then they began to appear in the eighteenth century and gained some popularity as the nineteenth century progressed. George Eliot was wont to split an occasional infinitive, as too was that very model of linguistic propriety, Henry James.

And now they are a perfectly valid option for English speakers to take. In fact, there are times when the splitting of an infinitive is not only completely acceptable but necessary, with its own specific meaning. Take this example: 'She decided to gradually get rid of the teddy bears she had collected.'[16] Try moving that 'gradually' to some-where else in the sentence and you'll find that you can't do it without changing the sense. The only way not to split that infinitive is to change the verb or rejig the sentence, e.g., 'She decided she would gradually get rid of . . .' or 'She decided to get rid of her teddy bear collection gradually.'

Nevertheless, split infinitives have been demonised, and the responsibility for that lies with one man, the hugely popular and completely barking Victorian grammarian Henry Alford, who attacked the increasingly trendy split infinitive in his *Plea for the Queen's English*, published in 1864. A handful of other grammarians then seized on something to condemn and ban and promptly condemned and banned it. Perhaps Alford objected to the split infinitive because it was a newish and still-developing usage. Perhaps he flinched because infinitives are often split in emphatic speech. Perhaps the trend was particularly popular with lower-class speak-ers. Perhaps it was nothing more than Alford obeying his own linguistic whim. Who knows? Not Henry Alford, who stated simply that 'to' and the verb were inseparable and that was that.

Which is, linguistically speaking, poppycock. Word order is very important in English, but the language retains a degree of flexibility so that words which go together grammatically don't always have to appear next to each other in a sentence. (The most obvious example is the splitting of a noun and its article. We combine 'the' + 'tasty' + 'pie' to form 'the tasty pie'. What's that then? A split nominative?)

Oddly enough, these Victorian grammarians were rumbled very quickly. In their highly influential guide, *The King's English*, published in 1907, the Fowler brothers condemn Alford's ban on the split infin-itive as 'a curious superstition'. After that, something even more

---

16   R. L. Trask, *Mind the Gaffe* (Penguin, 2002), pp. 269–70.

curious happens, with grammarians agreeing that although there was no valid reason not to split infinitives in English, they should remain unsplit because of the allegedly overwhelming but daft and fuddy-duddy prejudice against them. (Which has been commonly assumed to be the result of the mistaken influence of Latin grammar. In fact, Alford & Co. didn't refer to Latin, and the supposed Latin effect is only ever mentioned by people who go on to disagree with it and lament it. In any case, it makes no sense, because Latin infinitives come in single words.)

However, although it's arrant nonsense, and usually agreed to be so, the no-split-infinitives regulation is still established, even if only as a snippet of allegedly sage but actually wrong but still unacceptable grammatical truth. Split infinitives are still banned, but most often by people who accept that this ban is silly but who also know that it exists and who expect literate people to abide by it.

So split infinitives are still best avoided, especially in formal contexts, where they can be judged to be a sign of dirty-fingernailed illiteracy. It makes no sense, everyone knows it makes no sense, but it's still best not to use them in that company report or that exam paper. Avoid splits by (1) putting negatives before infinitives ('not to see', 'never to tell') and (2) keeping adverbs well away from the vicinity of any wandering infinitive or (3) just dispensing with the adverb (if in doubt, run away).

Gerunds

Argh. Like algebra and where to find the smokers' den, the gerund is one of those things which you thank the Lord you just don't need to bother about after you leave school. Or perhaps that dates my schooldays to the era of black-and-white TV when gerunds were still talked about openly. I suspect that they have seemed so intimidating that most teachers since those olden days have tried their best to pretend they don't exist.

I'm not going to pretend that gerunds aren't complicated in English. Because they can be very complicated indeed. Fiendishly so. But be of good cheer. You already have a perfect command of gerunds. You may not have a clue what they are but you know how to use them like you know how to eat.

Gerunds are verbs acting as nouns. When verbs do that in English, they take the same form as the present participle, with '-ing' at the end: 'cooking', 'booking', 'looking', 'going', 'being', 'trying', etc., etc. So, for example, when a verb follows a preposition, which requires a noun, the verb goes into its nouny gerund form – 'He was set on going to Skegness'; 'I look forward to hearing from you' (with all of us intuitively recognising that 'to' as a preposition rather than the start of an infinitive, because none of us would ever say, as an EFL student might, 'I look forward to hear from you'). But this '-ing' form doesn't appear only after prepositions; verbs become nouns as gerunds a lot. 'Cooking was my first love.' 'The centre-back was given a booking.' 'He actually enjoys shopping.'

Notice that third example; it's different from the other two where the verb-turned-noun is acting as a straightforward noun. In place of 'cooking' in 'Cooking was my first love', you could slip in another noun in its place – 'Debbie', 'Latvia', 'Jesus', or, to quote from the execrable song by John Miles, 'music' – and cause no grammatical damage.

But with the chap who 'enjoys shopping', 'shopping' follows another verb, 'enjoy'. When one verb follows another in English, the second verb usually goes into the infinitive – 'They hurried to catch their flight'; 'I'm going to biff you on the nose'; 'She works to support her wastrel husband.'

However, when some verbs, such as 'enjoy', are followed by another verb, the second verb takes not the infinitive but the gerundive '-ing' form. There is no reason or need for this; it's just one of those whims of a language, whose only apparent purpose is to mess with the heads of any adult trying to learn it.

This gerund business comes as a real dead-mouse-in-the-shoe surprise to EFL students, especially when they reach the bit coming up about gerund/infinitive alternatives. Well, straightforward though our grammar is, even English can conjure up a few unnecessary and brain-numbingly perplexing grammatical flourishes. French has those extremely annoying verbs that take 'être' instead of 'avoir', Spanish has its subjunctives, and English has its phrasal verbs and its verbs that take gerunds.

Here are the verbs that must be followed by verbs as gerunds:

admit	anticipate	appreciate	avoid
consider	defer	delay	deny
detest	dislike	dread	enjoy
excuse	finish	forgive	imagine
involve	keep	loathe	mind
miss	pardon	postpone	practise
prevent	resent	resist	risk
suggest	understand		

A few of these verbs, like 'admit' and 'understand', can also be followed by 'that' and then a verb, but none of them can be followed by infinitives. 'He enjoys to shop'. That's a real grammatical mistake, in any dialect of English, because 'enjoy' + gerund is a rule common to all English variants, so that when that rule isn't followed, it sounds plain wrong.

Verbs taking gerunds is bad enough but there's a twist coming up which makes EFL students put their heads in their hands and moan softly. Some verbs can take both infinitives and gerunds. And some – not all, but some – of these verbs do so with (that noise in the background is an advanced-level EFL student whimpering) an often subtle but always noticeable change of meaning.

Here are the verbs which can take either infinitives or gerunds:

advise	agree	allow	begin
cease	continue	forget	hate
intend	like	love	mean
need	permit	prefer	propose
recommend	regret	remember	require
start	stop	try	used to
want			

Let's start with an 'easy' one: 'mean'. Usually, 'mean' is followed by an infinitive – 'Do you mean to say that you've eaten all 365 of them?' However, if 'mean' means 'involve' in an impersonal construction starting with a determiner or 'it', then it takes a gerund – 'This will mean digging up the entire road.' Another fairly straightforward one is 'propose'. If it means 'intend' then it's usually followed by an infinitive – 'They proposed to go on strike' – but if it is used to mean the forwarding of a suggestion, then the gerund hoves into view –'She was hoping for Paris, but he proposed spending a fortnight in Skegness.'

Now let's tackle 'try'. 'Try' can take infinitives – 'try to leave', 'try to levitate' – or gerunds – 'try leaving', 'try levitating' – but there's a slight shift in meaning. 'Try' is followed by an infinitive when you know an attempt has been made but you don't know if it was successful. 'Try' takes a gerund when the attempt was successful but you don't know if it has had the desired effect. It may sound daftly perplexing but it's a rule we all follow. Look at the difference between 'He tried to lose weight' (probably without success but that's not certain and the sentence could still feasibly continue, 'and did very well, getting down to twelve stone': you just don't know the result) versus 'He tried losing weight' (and implicitly succeeded), but it's the effect that's important, so now the sentence would have to continue along the lines of 'and he still felt depressed'.

Now for a group of four verbs: 'advise', 'recommend', 'allow' and 'permit'. As you don't know you know, each of these is followed by a gerund when there is no specific mention of anyone being advised, recommended, allowed or permitted. ('We really recommend going on the London Eye'; 'He doesn't allow smoking in his car'.) However, these four verbs have to be followed by an infinitive if (a) there is a mention of the person on the receiving end ('I advised him to take echinacea'; 'They recommended us to try the place next door') or (b) it's in the negative ('You're not allowed to smoke here'; 'The tourists were not advised to avoid bandit country'). Try any of these examples with gerunds and they'll all sound wrong, because although they're arcane and complicated, these are hard and fast rules.

And now it's time to move on to a trio of verbs which can really bamboozle EFL students: 'regret', 'remember' and 'forget'. Here's their rule: 'regret', 'remember' and 'forget' take gerunds when the action happened before the regretting, remembering or forgetting, and infinitives when the action is to follow. Take this pair – 'He remembered switching off the oven' versus 'He remembered to switch off the oven'. With the gerund – 'He remembered switching off . . .' – he had the memory of having done something earlier. With the infinitive – 'He remembered to switch off . . .' – he did the remembering first and then the switching off. You can see the same rule in this depressing pair: 'I regret telling you . . .' (first the telling, then the regretful second thoughts) versus 'I regret to tell you . . .' (first the regretting, then the bad news). It sounds complicated. And that's because it is, if you think about it, which English learners have to. Yet we obey this rule without giving it the least thought as we prattle on.

I have come across one solitary example of a native speaker getting this rule wrong, and it's so odd that I've puzzled over it for many years, such is my rich and thrilling inner life. The native speaker committing the grammatical offence was John Betjeman, when he started a review of Kingsley Amis's *Lucky Jim* with the following sentence: 'I do not remember to have read a funnier first novel since Evelyn Waugh's *Decline and Fall* . . .'[17] 'I do not remember to have read . . .' Eh? It has to be 'I do not remember having read . . .' Surely?

My best guess is this: either a subeditor miscorrected the original or John Betjeman got into a bit of a tizz writing that sentence, but either the sub or the future poet laureate must have considered 'I do not remember having read', dismissed that because that could mean he'd suffered a memory lapse, and opted finally for 'I do not remember to have read' on the grounds that it probably was the proper and correct form because it sounded stilted, just like other supposedly impeccably 'correct' forms such as 'It is I' and 'smaller than she'.

Finally, my own personal favourite: 'like'. This friendly, unassuming and completely regular little verb turns into a horrible wee grammatical gremlin when it comes up against other verbs. In a conditional form, 'like' is usually followed by an infinitive ('I would like to pay for the window he broke'), but a gerund is often used if the thing being liked is being discussed in the abstract ('He'd like cooking if he would only learn'). In other tenses, 'like' + verb-turned-into-gerund indicates enjoyment, whereas 'like' + infinitive means that something is beneficial or wise to do, with enjoyment not an issue. 'I like eating ice-cream' ('like' plus gerund because I like the taste of ice-cream). 'I like to eat ice-cream' (like plus infinitive because the ice-cream is somehow good for me, so I'm probably recovering from a tonsillectomy). 'I like to go to the dentist twice a year' (yes indeed, but I don't like going). 'I like going to the dentist' (I've just revealed that I fancy my dentist).

---

17   John Betjeman, 'Amusing Story of Life at a Provincial University', *Daily Telegraph*, 5 February 1954, p. 8.

8 Adverbs

Like adjectives, adverbs are describing words. But whereas adjectives describe nouns, adverbs describe other sorts of word. They can describe verbs ('The alcoholic stumbled *uncertainly* into the shop'), they can describe adjectives ('where he bought an *unfeasibly* large bottle of cider for an *amazingly* cheap £1.99'), and they can describe other adverbs ('*very* luckily for him because he was in an estate agent's').

English adverbs are usually formed simply by adding '-ly' to the end of an adjective. That's the rule, as fundamental as it is obvious, in all traditional grammar manuals – although it is, to use one of those manuals' favourite terms, a howler. 'Adverbs add an "-ly"' is a formula that applies, some of the time, to just one dialect: standard English. In all other dialects of English, adverbs usually take the same form as adjectives – 'He drives slow'; 'She speaks awful quiet'; 'They're behaving real strange'; 'The boy done good.'

Before anyone assigns the non-standard dialects' lack of an '-ly' in adverbs to the innate laziness of the great unwashed, it's worth pointing out that standard English is the only dialect of all the Germanic languages and dialects where adverbs differ from adjectives. There's nothing wrong with -ly-less adverbs and we accept them quite happily when they crop up, as they often do, in idioms ('Kiss me quick') and song titles ('Love Me Tender', 'Need Your Love So Bad'), where standard forms with '-ly' would sound as daft as the proper version of the Rolling Stones line as recommended by Brian Jones's dad – 'I can't get any satisfaction'.

Even in standard English, lots of words don't add '-ly' when they become adverbs. Understandably, those that already end in '-ly' tend not to add a second: 'kindly' and 'daily', 'weekly', 'monthly' and 'yearly'. 'Silly' also, although 'sillily' does make it into the *Oxford English Dictionary* where it's marked as 'rare'. As for most other adjectives that already end in '-ly' – 'early', 'deadly', 'friendly', 'likely', 'lonely' – standard English gives up and doesn't use them as adverbs, getting round the problem of potential '-lily' tongue-twisting by opting for a longer-winded phrase such as 'in a friendly way' instead.

Other words that are the same in standard English whether they're working as adjectives or adverbs are 'ill', 'well' (as in good health), 'still', 'back', 'fast', 'long' and 'straight' and directional terms ('right', 'left', 'north', 'south', 'east' and 'west'). There's no reason why they shouldn't, but 'straightly', 'longly', 'leftly', 'southly', etc. don't exist.

'Leftly' may not be acceptable but 'rightly' is – except that 'rightly' belongs to a subset of adverbs which have shifted meaning since they were adjectives. Some adjectives of temperature and measurement become adverbs about emotions and attitudes ('cold', 'hot', 'warm', 'cool') or abstractions ('deep', 'high'). Others just shift meaning.

The following are words that have different meanings as adjectives and adverbs (they appear with standard-English '-ly' because the different form makes things clearer, and because this is a book):

late	lately	= recently
near	nearly	= almost
short	shortly	= soon
fair	fairly	= unenthusiastic modifier
hard	hardly	= indicating scarcety, paucity, near
bare	barely	failure, mostly used in negative constructions

Hence the difference between 'You've barely seen her' and 'You've seen her bare'. 'Hard' presents another complication, because it can work as an adverb without changing form, when it retains its adjectival meaning – as in 'Working hard? Or hardly working?'

'Fairly' and 'barely' also belong to a tricky group of qualifiers, along with 'rather', 'pretty' and 'quite'. As an adjective, 'pretty' means good-looking, with an adverbial form in standard English of 'prettily'. But 'pretty' is also an adverb, when it acts as a positive reinforcer, with a strength equivalent to or just short of 'very'. 'Fairly' and 'rather' both mean moderately or partly, 'fairly' usually being paired with positive words, 'rather' mainly before negatives, although that needn't be the case, and much depends on context and emphasis – 'She's rather lovely', a roué might say approvingly, although that roué would most probably be saying that in a posh accent, possibly while wearing red trousers. 'Quite' plays a dual role. It's usually a modifier unless it occurs with extreme adjectives in which case it's a reinforcer: hence the faint praise of 'quite clever' versus the enthusiasm of 'quite brilliant', 'quite nice' versus 'quite marvellous'.

Generally, though, extreme adjectives are qualified by extreme adverbs, gradable adjectives with modifying ones: 'completely wonderful', 'utterly horrendous', 'absolutely fabulous', but 'very good', 'fairly warm' and 'rather cold'. Swap those around and they just don't sound right. At least, that's how they're said to work in EFL manuals and how they work for me, but some others don't seem to make such a clear distinction. Geoffrey Sampson, for example: casting an eye over his own work at the end of the second chapter of *The 'Language Instinct' Debate*, he reaches the fortunate conclusion that it is 'very complete in its analysis'.

Adverbs can come in comparative and superlative forms. In standard, the few single-syllable adverbs like 'hard' take '-er' and '-est', as does 'early'. Almost all the others are preceded by 'more' and 'most'. 'More' and 'most' are themselves two of the few irregular adverbs in standard, being the comparative and superlatives of 'much'. The others are 'well', 'better', 'best'; 'badly', 'worse', 'worst'; 'little', 'less', 'least'; and 'far', 'further', 'furthest'.

In line with that stipulation about only gradable adjectives taking gradable, modifying adverbs, the rule in standard, and especially written English, is that extreme adverbs can't take comparative and superlative forms. However, as the example in Chapter 5 shows, the ban on constructions like 'most perfect' and 'most perfectly' is a relatively recent one.

Although they are usually fairly easy to spot in standard English with their tell-tale '-ly' ending, there are some adverbs which are more difficult to identify. Often, this is because they just lack an '-ly' form, as with a word like 'often', an adverb of frequency. Other frequency adverbs are 'seldom', 'sometimes', 'never', 'once' and 'twice'; those of time are 'soon', 'then', 'after' and 'now'. They may not sound like adverbs but they occupy the same role in statements as '-ly' words such as 'occasionally' or 'regularly'. For example: 'She always adds carrots to spaghetti bolognese but the kids never eat them.'

Other unadverby-sounding adverbs include those referring to direction and place: 'He's gone abroad without telling me so I reckon this marriage is heading south.' 'Here' and 'there', 'everywhere' and 'anywhere', 'near' and 'far' can all be adverbs. So too can words that are normally prepositions like 'in' and 'out', 'up' and 'down' – 'I think I'll go up to the lingerie department'; 'I see the pound has gone down against the dollar.' They don't look like adverbs but they are describing the verbs in their sentences: so 'immediately' or 'badly', for example, could replace them without any grammatical hitch. Even nouns can take on an adverbial role. Take a personal catchphrase, 'I'll do it tomorrow': that last word might not sound like an adverb, and it isn't an adverb in statements like 'Tomorrow is another day', 'Tomorrow never dies' or 'All tomorrow's parties' where it's a noun, but in my catchphrase it's an adverb, as you'll see if you replace it with a conventional (standard) '-ly' word like 'quickly' or 'incompetently'.

Coping as bravely as they can with grammar's fuzziness, most manuals also lump a couple of other groups of words into their adverb sections (see below). One group contains those words we use to introduce statements, like 'also', 'however', 'moreover', 'therefore', 'besides'. Another group consists of words which also usually start statements, to describe the attitude or opinion of the speaker, for example 'possibly', 'maybe' or 'arguably'.

By far the most controversial adverb of recent times has been another member of the attitude-marking group: poor old 'hopefully'. This word has shifted its role and meaning, from being an adverb of manner, meaning 'full of hope' – 'She bought a scratch card hopefully'; 'He kicked the ball hopefully' – to become a sentence-starter meaning 'I hope that' – 'Hopefully, she's remembered to pack her sunhat'; 'Hopefully, the glazier can come first thing tomorrow'.

A small shift, and a modest one, but this new use has been met with fierce resistance and the contemptuous scorn of traditionalists, like Kingsley Amis: 'When someone says or writes, "Hopefully, the plan will be in operation by the end of the year", we know immediately that we are dealing with a dimwit at best.'[1] But actually this new use of 'hopefully' has proved very popular because it works so neatly and effectively. Anyway, the signs are that the resistance is nearly over, with sentence-starting attitudinal 'hopefully' coming to be seen as just about acceptable – in conversation at least, although most subeditors and many old-school teachers start twitching at this newer use of 'hopefully' and eagerly redpencil it as just wrong, wrong, wrong. It isn't, of course, but good luck with telling them that.

---

1 Kingsley Amis, *The King's English* (HarperCollins, 1997), p. 158.

Not only do our adverbs come in a variety of actually separate functions but, as if designed specifically to confuse EFL students, they vary widely in the positions they can take up. This habit of adverbs to dot about the place causes even us native speakers problems when we write and suddenly find ourselves with an 'urgently' or a 'fortunately' on our hands and uncertain where to put it.

Here are some of the problems posed by our adverbs' placements.

Adverbs of frequency can shift around quite happily, occasionally conveying a slight change of emphasis or meaning – 'He visits his old mum often'; 'He often visits his old mum'; 'Often, he visits his old mum'. However, with simple tenses of the verb 'to be', they usually go after the verb – 'He is often over at his old mum's.'

Adverbs of manner usually appear after the verb if there's no object ('He kicked ineptly') or after the object if there is one ('He kicked the ball ineptly') except if there's a more extended phrase after the verb in which case the adverb usually shifts to come before the verb ('He ineptly kicked the ball straight at the window and broke the damned thing'). The one place that adverb can't go is between the verb and the object ('He kicked ineptly the ball'). If the construction is a verb + preposition + object, the adverb goes either before the preposition or after the object ('He kicked ineptly at the ball'; 'He kicked at the ball ineptly') unless the object's a long phrase, when the adverb really has to come before the preposition ('He kicked ineptly at the ball which the dog had just been chewing'). A dry paragraph, I have to admit, but imagine just how appalling, how mind-numbing and spirit-breaking such explanations must be to someone concentrating hard on their *Let's Speak English for Business* volume 2.

Adverbs of degree – 'almost', 'barely', 'entirely', 'hardly', 'nearly', 'only', 'quite', 'rather', 'really' and 'scarcely' – are slotted in before the adjective or adverb they're going with ('You're rather upset' 'Well, I was almost asleep – it is really late'), with the exception of 'enough', which must follow the word it's qualifying – 'This town ain't big enough for both of us.' However, when an adverb of degree accompanies a verb, it has to be placed in front of it – 'That little boy almost kicked the ball into that policeman's groin.'

In written English, a particular problem is presented by 'only', which has to go before the word it's paired with, even though it dodges about quite contentedly in our conversations – 'I only shagged him once' in written English would be taken by sticklers to say that the action of shagging was of no importance, so unless that really was the intended meaning, the order sticklers would accept is 'I shagged him only once'.

Word order

Some of English's adverbs, in all dialects, standard and non-standard alike, have a curious trick of inverting the usual word order – mainly with negatives and usually with some small degree of drama – 'Barely had they got there . . .' 'Scarcely had he reached it . . .' – and occasionally making it difficult not to sound like a bit of a pompous old twerp ('Never/seldom/rarely' have I had the misfortune to . . .'). Handy for a certain sort of schoolteacher, I suppose, and quite popular with the kind of people who get worked up about the ways other people talk.

A similar inversion can happen after some adverbs indicating direction: 'away', 'up', 'down', 'out' and 'in', etc. An example which I offer freely to the cricket-going public with a peak 78.9 per cent applicability at the start of the season is 'Down came the rain, off went the players so out came our sandwiches. And cakes.'

If we're including them as adverbs of direction, as most grammars do, then it's time to mention 'here' and 'there', which can also invert their following words: 'Here Griselda is' is possible but more common is 'Here is Griselda.' Some idioms follow English's usual SV order – 'Here we go', 'Here I am', 'Here it is' – but in some other idioms, usually after 'be', 'come' and 'go', the verb and subject noun swap to follow a VS model – 'There goes the neighbourhood'; 'Here is the news'; 'There's Paul McCartney!' This is much less available if pronouns are involved – 'Here comes she!' isn't on. But if there's no pronoun, it is often the only option – 'Here comes Griselda!' This confused my six-year-old son after he obeyed the usual subject–verb sequence – 'Here Mum comes,' he said. 'Is that right?' he asked after a pause, then thought about it for a moment. 'Yes. Here Mum comes,' he repeated, uneasily.

Some adverbs that refer to human attributes – 'cleverly', 'intelligently', 'stupidly', 'foolishly', 'sweetly', 'generously' – can take up different positions in the sentence, i.e., at the start, before verbs, after verbs, and right at the end, after verbs + objects. With some – not all, but some – of these changes of position there is a change of meaning. Baffling no doubt for the *Let's Speak English!* readership but for us graspable with a couple of examples.

(1) 'Crazily, I answered the policeman.' 'I crazily answered the policeman.' Both positions are possible and both refer to the ill-advised fact of giving an answer when you should have kept quiet or demanded to see a lawyer. However, 'I answered the policeman crazily'; that refers to the mad quality of the answer, when you told him your name was Jimothy Ovencleaner and explained that invisible aliens were to blame.

(2) 'Stupidly, she wrote it down.' 'She stupidly wrote it down.' The act of writing something down was stupid, so what she was writing had to be something like the phone number of the person she was having an affair with. 'She wrote it down stupidly' – she didn't understand what she was writing, she got the wrong end of the stick or she just came up with stupid stuff.

(3) 'Generously, he paid for the meal.' 'He generously paid for the meal.' That was nice of him, the 'generously' referring to the act of

paying. But 'He paid for the meal generously' – he gave a sum of money above the going rate, 'generously' referring to the payment itself.

Adverbs that describe attitude at the start of sentences – 'fortunately', 'honestly', 'frankly', 'luckily', etc. – can also move to the usual, later slots, but with a change in meaning, because they undergo the same shift back to the original quality instead of the attitude. Try moving the adverb around in 'Naturally, she fed the baby' or 'Honestly, I didn't do it'.

Now, I have to concede that this chapter seems to be dying on its feet, and with not too much raging against the dying of the light that I can see . . . but there's little I can do about it. If this chapter seems to the unkind eye to have almost no dignity left, that's adverbs' fault, not mine. Adverbs are the hardest of the word classes to summarise because they're the fuzziest and the most shapeless, bulging out in some awkward places where it's hard to fit in a lot of awkward words. Adverbs have been used like the cupboard under the stairs – somewhere to put a lot of very different items that are all useful but not easily kept in the normal shelving.

9 Prepositions

'*Beside* the table', '*under* the roof', '*in* the cupboard', '*before* teatime', '*after* the incident'; as in these examples, prepositions usually go with nouns, usually before nouns, and usually to locate those nouns in space or time. They can also specify the relationship between words – 'I gave it *to* you'; 'She made it *for* him'.

In languages with lots of different case endings, the nouns would change form in all those examples to show what they were doing or what was happening to them. In uninflected English, prepositions do the work instead and the words they're specifying don't change. Our prepositions stay the same too, unlike, say, Irish, where they shift form according to person, gender and number, so that 'do' ('to') appears in the singular as 'dom' ('to me'), 'duit' ('to you'), 'dó' ('to him or it') and 'di' ('to her').[1]

We use prepositions a lot, in fact three of the six most commonly used words in English are prepositions:

the	(definite article)
of	(preposition)
and	(conjunction)

---

1 Where do prepositions come from? In *The Unfolding of Language*, Guy Deutscher shows how many are derived from nouns for parts of the body, first to locate something in space, then in time and finally as an abstract notion. Take the pert example of 'behind', which starts out as a tush (from the OE for rear-end, hind), becomes three different types of preposition – as in 'it's behind you!', 'we're behind time', and 'I'm behind with the rent' – and then returns as a metonymic noun for the most prominent bit of you that's behind you.

to	(preposition)
a	(indefinite article)
in	(preposition)

The top ten most used prepositions are: 'of', 'to', 'in', 'for', 'on', 'with', 'as', 'by', 'at', 'from'.

As they are in almost every other language, English's prepositions tend to be very short.

As with almost every component of every language, there are a few exceptions to the rule with English's prepositions but only a handful of exceptions to only one rule; the one about word order. Our prepositions always come before nouns, except for a few which come after (so that they're properly termed postpositions): 'ago', 'apart', and 'aside'. (Also, sometimes, 'through' and, also sometimes but not very often at all, 'notwithstanding'.)

Prepositions in English may not get up to any grammatical tricks but they can still be very, very hard for adult learners to get right, because their own languages will often have different prepositions than English for the same situation. Take a basic spatial preposition, 'on'. Steven Pinker notes that English can have a book on a table, a picture hanging on a wall, and a ring worn on a finger, where our neighbour and cousin Dutch has a different preposition for each: 'op' for a book on a table, 'aan' for a picture on a wall, and 'om' for a ring on a finger.[2]

As if that were not bad enough, our prepositions pair up with adjectives and (you may just hear violins starting quietly with high, *Psycho* shower-scene staccato chords) verbs in most particular ways.

Adjectives first. 'I'm really sorry X the dreadful mess.' 'You're keen X him'. 'He's proud X his daughters.' You know the answers because you've unknowingly learned just about every combination

---

2   Steven Pinker, *The Stuff of Thought* (Allen Lane, 2007), pp. 177–9 and 182–3.

of adjective + preposition English can come up with. But for adult learners they can be very difficult to get right. (For us natives too, going by the unabashed, have-a-go-and-see-if-it-sounds-okay mistakes children occasionally make – 'I'm very interested about dinosaurs'; 'I'm sorry of the mess'.)

Some verbs also require specific prepositions: we apologise 'to' someone 'for' something; we are told to beware 'of' the dog; we hope 'for' and insist 'on' the best; we rely 'on' each other and believe 'in' ghosts. There are lots of those and each one has to be learned – unconsciously and, a few childhood mistakes apart, with marvellous ease and mastery if you're us; with great effort and difficulty if English isn't your first language.

But that's just the start of it with verbs + prepositions. Because now, as *Psycho* shower-scene violins jag ever louder, we come to a part of our grammar that is guaranteed to break the spirit of even the most stout-hearted EFL students, although it's one we're about to prance through. You probably aren't aware of their existence but you use them all the time, there are thousands of them, and they are the bane of English learners the world over. They are the verbs and prepositions that combine to make – cue full volume on the staccato violins – phrasal verbs.

A phrasal verb is the result of a preposition joining a verb to function together as a new verb – one which has a new meaning, which is usually completely unpredictable, often specific, and frequently accompanied by other completely unpredictable meanings for the same verb + preposition combination. That's why they are so massively unpopular with adult learners; they form a huge subclass of words that exist beyond the rule of any linguistic law, free to wander and roam and do whatever they damn well please, as untameable and about as unlearnable as a language can get.

Take 'look + up' for example: this can work conventionally, of course, as the ordinary verb 'look' plus 'up' acting as a normal directional preposition – 'I told you not to look up his kilt'. However, 'look up' can also mean 'visit' ('If you're ever down in Texas, look me up'), 'consult in a reference book/facility' ('She looked it up on Wikipedia'), and, as long as the subject is a nebulous concept such as life or business, 'improve' ('Things are looking up'). There's also 'look up to', meaning admire and respect, as well as 'look (someone) up and down' in its sense of assessment.

'Up' and 'up to' are just two of the many prepositions that combine with 'look' to form phrasal verbs. There's also 'look after', 'look ahead', 'look at', 'look back', 'look back on', 'look down on', 'look for', 'look forward to', 'look in', 'look into', 'look on', 'look on to', 'look out', 'look out for', and 'look over'.

There are a dozen or so other verbs like 'look' that take a lot of different prepositions, frequently with multiple meanings: 'be', 'break', 'call', 'come', 'get', 'go', 'make', 'put', 'run', 'take' and 'turn' are the worst offenders with each taking a host of 'fors' and 'afters' and 'intos' and 'outs'. But many, many verbs can take several prepositions, and many of those many more than several. For example, the not terribly common verb 'lay' can form seven different phrasal verbs with 'away', 'down', 'in', 'into', 'on', 'off' and 'out'.

One online guide boasts that it explains 2,931 phrasal verbs, from 'account for' to the four phrasal verbs using 'zoom' ('zoom in', 'zoom in on', 'zoom off' and 'zoom out'). And that's just a basic guide. There are about 6,000 phrasal verbs catalogued in their very own Oxford dictionary. It's called *The Oxford Dictionary of Phrasal Verbs*, and as any English learner will attest, the title is the only straightforward thing about it.

Even worse for EFL learners, there's no getting round them. We use phrasal verbs a lot and keep on making more of them. So it's impossible to say how many phrasal verbs there are exactly, because we native speakers are rather into ('to be + into' = to be enthusiastic about) them, and add new ones, like 'to be into', all the time. Another recent example is the increasing popularity of the (I think) originally Liverpudlian 'make' + 'up' meaning to be very happy. Thus confusing even further the already bewildering entry for 'make + up' which already had six completely separate meanings: to decide ('He made up his mind'), to lie or invent ('He made up an excuse'), to apply cosmetics to a face ('She's going to make herself up'), to consist of ('The army was made up of conscripts'), to mix or assemble ('The chemist made up the prescription'), and to be reconciled ('They kissed and made up').

As the various meanings of 'make + up' show, the usually Anglo-Saxon-based phrasal verbs can often be translated into more high-falutin', Latin- or French-based words – 'compensate', 'consist', 'to be reconciled', etc. – so a favourite tactic of EFL students is to use the more polysyllabic alternative. Native speakers do this too, if we suspect that the phrasal verb sounds a bit too Anglo-Saxony colloquial. Hence the British Rail verb for leaving a train – not 'get out' but 'alight'. (Alight? When, in all honesty, have you ever used the verb 'alight'?) 'Alight here for connections to Manchester . . .' It may be a strange verb for us to cope with, but how much worse for non-natives, left to flick hastily through their dictionaries while under the vague impression that they've just been told to set themselves on fire.

To make matters even more fiendish, there's the basic anarchy of phrasal verbs to cope with. Not only do EFL learners have to memorise the random and often multiple and often highly specific meanings of each phrasal verb, they also have to learn how each one operates; whether it's transitive or intransitive, and if it's transitive, where to put the preposition.

If a verb is transitive that means that it can take an object – 'He stole the money' ('stole', verb, + object, 'the money'). If a verb is intransitive it can't take an object, like the Liverpudlian 'make + up' or, say, 'make off', in the sense of performing a getaway – 'He stole the money then made off.' You can't add an object noun or noun phrase after that 'off'; another prepositional phrase maybe, like 'into the night', or 'on a motorbike', but not an object ('he made off the . . .' doesn't work).

Alas for EFL learners, the same phrasal verb can be transitive or intransitive, depending on its meaning. For instance, 'make out' transitively means to see with some degree of exertion or difficulty; as an intransitive in the USA, it means to canoodle.

There's more. Those phrasal verbs that can be followed by an object (the transitive ones) then subdivide into those where the object has to follow the preposition and those where the object can either follow the preposition or come between the verb and the preposition. Except when the object is a pronoun, in which case it must come before the preposition. Confused? Not in real life, you're not, where you happily vary between 'I took off my clothes' and 'I took my clothes off' but you would automatically say, 'I took them off' and spurn 'I took off them'. Similarly, we would never say, 'I looked it at' or 'I made up it' or 'She went him off'.

An example of Johnny Foreigner not quite getting this rule comes from the Norwegian band A-ha and their smash hit of 1985, 'Take on me'. Distracted by the synths, a strange, semi-animated video, and singer Morten Harket's extraordinary cheekbones and falsetto, the British public happily accepted 'Take on me', passing over the oddness of the song's title – odd because the rule for the phrasal verb 'take + on' is that it places the pronoun between the two components (except, I suppose, in very unusual cases where the pronoun would be very emphatically emphasised: 'He's going to take on *me*?'). Also, what exactly do the lyrics mean? 'Take on me. Take me on . . .' – is Morten Harket inviting his beloved to fight him . . . or employ him perhaps? I suppose the grammatically acceptable 'take me on' does just about make sense, since 'take + on' can also mean 'accept responsibility for' – 'She took on a challenging job as head of PR for North

Korea' – in which case, 'take me on' could mean something like 'be in a relationship with me and be prepared to cope with all my emotional baggage', but as a chat-up line, it's a bit of a non-starter. Proving how awfully tricky phrasal verbs can be, 'take + on' also has a separate meaning when it's used intransitively – 'Oh, don't take on so'. Wise advice, as it happens, for the stricken Morten Harket, so strung out in his romantic urgings that he reaches a high E in each chorus. Despite, I'm afraid, the words, so fortunately hidden behind Morten Harket's falsetto shriek – 'Take on me. Take me on. I'll be gone. In a day or two.'

But phrasal verbs can flummox even the most able non-native speakers, such as the pretty well fluent Portuguese football manager, Andre Villas-Boas, who confidently went for a phrasal verb after he was turfed out of his job at Chelsea, and came up with one that doesn't exist when he accused the club's owner Roman Abramovich of 'not putting up to the things that he promised'. You what?

Specific behaviour patterns and unguessable meanings; it's no wonder most non-natives try to avoid them and why advanced EFL students so dread the phrasal verbs' multiple-choice exam: 'John didn't have his glasses so he couldn't make . . . the address.' Is it (A) 'on' (B) 'off' (C) 'out', or (D) 'over'?

Studied English at university? Lived in London for a year? Think you're pretty fluent? Have a flick through the *Oxford Dictionary of Phrasal Verbs*, Pablo/Akiko/François, and think again.

However, lest us natives or we natives get too smug, let's bear in mind the reign of terror wreaked on our own preposition usage by the staple old-school rule: never use a preposition with which to end a sentence. It's a quirk of traditional grammars to point out this rule, then to say it's crazy and then to say that other grammars seem to think it's a rule, so it had better be followed when possible.

Instructively, H. W. Fowler strenuously defends the option of leaving prepositions at the end of sentences if it feels right; or, more accurately, 'according to the impression it makes on the feeling of educated English readers'.

Well, it often does feel absolutely fine for us English speakers, no matter what exams we've passed, because, like the Scandinavian languages and a few west-African languages, English happily allows sentences to end with prepositions – 'It's the bag I came with'; 'That's the chair I sat on'. This is often particularly noticeable with questions – 'Are you going to see him off?' 'Which door did you go out of?'

Preposition-stranding is the technical term for this. It's not a particularly popular option among the world's languages, as witness that rather brief list of others that use it. But it's an option English takes. As in this one, we often use prepositions to end sentences with. And when we end a sentence with a phrasal verb, as we frequently do, we have no option but to leave a preposition dangling at the end – 'The boy kicked off'; 'The ball bounced up'; 'The glass crashed down'; 'The rest of us ran away'.

English not only allows stranded prepositions, it's really rather fond of them. So fond, in fact, that the quirk has rubbed off on some American and Canadian dialects of French, which usually loathes putting prepositions at the end. 'La fille qui je t'ai parlé de,' a New Orleans French speaker might say, to the processing stare of a French speaker from Orléans.

So English is obviously quite happy to place prepositions at the end of the sentence they're in. And avoiding that by shoving the preposition in earlier – together with a 'which' or even a 'whom', because you need an extra relative pronoun to indicate the thing the preposition was linked with originally – rarely sounds anything other than forced and affected and just too posh by half. Take the second half of the first sentence in this paragraph; how could we hoik that 'in' away from the end? – '. . . at the end of the sentence in which they are . . .'?

There's one man to blame for the random banning of stranded prepositions: John Dryden, or the poet John Dryden (1631–1700), to use his full title. He came to loathe sentence-final prepositions after he tested the purity of his English prose by translating it into Latin, then back into English, which of course had lots of prepositions that inflected Latin lacked. So the poet John Dryden (1631–1700) would rewrite his lines with lots of 'in whiches' and 'for whoms' to eradicate any danglers.[3] Obviously, the poet John Dryden (1631–1700) didn't know what he was talking about. Or, as the poet John Dryden (1631–1700) would have preferred, he didn't know about what he was talking.

Because it's a normal and often unavoidable part of English not to obey this completely invented rule, grammarians usually make a big fuss about being hip to the jive and allowing them to exist, and berating others who get all worked up about them and try to forbid them. Ernest Gowers, for example, in *The Complete Plain Words*, approvingly quotes Winston Churchill when he was corrected by some minion for a stranded preposition: 'This is the sort of English up with which I will not put.'[4] (Churchill's remark seems to have first appeared in Gowers's story, with no identified source and no corroboration, and it hasn't been mentioned in any of the many official biographies, so, famous and useful though the example is, I'm afraid it looks awfully like an urban legend.)

With an avuncular chuckle, Gowers also offers the anecdote that later linguists will often cite, about a nurse who enquired why a patient had borrowed a particular book from the hospital library: 'What did you choose that book to be read to out of for?'

3 Hitchings, *Language Wars*, pp. 58–60.

4 Ernest Gowers, *The Complete Plain Words* (rev. edn by Sidney Greenbaum and Janet Whitcut) (HMSO, 1986), p. 107.

Four stranded prepositions in a row. Excellent work. How on earth would the poet John Dryden (1631–1700) have gone about repositioning those? 'For what reason did you choose that book out of which . . .'.

10 Conjunctions

Conjunctions are joining words, like 'and' or 'but'. They can join items in pairs – 'fish and chips', 'Oliver and Hardy' – or in lists – 'Peter, Paul and Mary'; 'The good, the bad and the ugly'; 'The boy kicked, headed and caught the ball.' They can also join parts of a sentence together. There are two separate groups of these sentence-constructing conjunctions, with different functions.

Co-ordinating conjunctions These join equal parts of a sentence – 'The boy kicked the ball and the window shattered'; 'The boy kicked the ball, yet the ball hardly moved in the mud'; 'The boy kicked the ball but the ball had been punctured and badly chewed by his pet dachshund Bonzo.'

There are seven words in English which can do a co-ordinating conjunction's job: 'for', 'and', 'nor', 'but', 'or', 'yet' and 'so'. I give them in that order because they are sometimes known collectively as FANBOYS. (I'd have thought YOBFANS or BOYFANS would have been more memorable, and FABSONY might have earned a product-placement fee – but then again, why on earth would anyone need any mnemonic for the instant and reliable recall of the co-ordinating conjunctions?)

Subordinating conjunctions This group has many more members, which can be either single words or phrases:

after	although	as	at
because	before	beside(s)	between

by	despite	if	since
so	than	that	though
unless	until	when	where
while	with	without	

as if/though	as long/soon/much as	as well as
because of	due to	even if/though
in accordance with	in addition to	in case
in order that/to	in spite of	instead of
on account of	only if	owing to
provided that	so that	

These are termed subordinating conjunctions because when they link together parts of a sentence, the part they introduce is secondary or subordinate to the main part.

> The boy kicked the ball, [as if he were Ronaldo.]
> [Even though he knew it was an ill-advised move with so much glass nearby,] the boy kicked the ball.
> The boy kicked the ball repeatedly, [until the window broke.]
> [When the ball broke the window,] the boy ran off.
> The window broke [because that little bastard kicked a ball at it.]

These subordinating conjunctions signal a variety of different contexts or meanings, the most usual being a time sequence ('after', 'before', 'when', etc.), a reason ('because', 'as', 'since'), a concession ('although', 'despite', 'while'), a condition ('if', 'even if', 'unless'), a purpose ('in order that/to', 'so') and a result ('so', 'so that'). As in most of the examples above, it's often possible to swap the order of the two parts of the sentence round and keep the grammar and meaning intact.

There are many items in those lists of subordinating conjunctions which may seem familiar from Chapter 9 on prepositions. Indeed, they are labelled 'conjunctive prepositions' in the *Oxford Modern English Grammar*. The linked but slightly different functions of a word like 'after' can be seen in the following examples: 'The boy ran after the ball' (preposition, going with 'the ball'); 'The boy ran off after the accident' (preposition, going with 'the accident'); 'The boy ran off after the window broke' (conjunction, linking the main part of the sentence – 'the boy ran off' – with the subordinate one, 'the window broke').

The traditional grammars can usually muster up only one rule with conjunctions; that co-ordinating conjunctions, especially 'and', can't begin sentences. Actually, as with prepositions dangling at the end of sentences, many traditional grammarians like to undo a couple of buttons of their girdles and shake their hair loose at this point. First they make sure to cite the rule against starting sentences with an 'And' or a 'But'. Then they make a real show of pooh-poohing this as a fuddy-duddy regulation. Then they daringly unban it, explaining that 'And' or 'But' at the start of a sentence can have a certain rhetorical force, if used wisely and sparingly. Wow! Matron's doing the twist.

For once, the original regulation wasn't modelled on Latin – where, because of the flexibility of the word order in a case-marked system, 'et' could easily turn up at the start of a sentence ('Et tu, Brute'). Rather, the no-ands-at-the-start rule was presumably invented to stop the naive, childlike sequencing of 'And then . . . And then . . . And then . . .'

But what to make of the Bible? Particularly in the Old Testament, the basic 'And then . . . And then' constructions aren't just a rhetorical option used wisely and sparingly. Particularly in the earlier books of the Old Testament, with very infrequent exceptions, the 'And' + simple declaration is the only sentence structure used. Here, taken pretty well at random, are the first few verses of chapter 4 of Exodus:

> And Moses answered and said, 'But behold, they will not believe me, nor hearken unto my voice; for they will say, "The Lord hath not appeared unto thee."' And the Lord said unto him, 'What is that in thine hand?' And he said, 'A rod.' And He said, 'Cast it on the ground.' And he cast it on the ground, and it became a serpent; and Moses fled from before it. And the Lord said unto Moses, 'Put forth thine hand, and take it by the tail.' And he put forth his hand, and caught it, and it became a rod in his hand.

Granted, this style does suit the Bible's mission, to declaim absolute truths with absolute authority. However, as adult prose it does read very oddly. A minor strangeness is the careless, confusing use of pronouns which don't obey our conventions, so that it's not clear from the grammar who is talking or what's happening ('Put forth thine hand, and take it by the tail'). But the main oddity, especially in the Old Testament, is the basic and basically unvarying sentence structure – a simple statement prefaced by an 'And', one following another in a declaimed list of events, with precious little variety in the grammar and nothing like a subordinate clause, not even a basic 'when X happened, then Y . . .' construction.

It's not just colours that are missing in the Old Testament but any sort of variety or any sort of development at all, really, in the sentence structure. As with colour words, this absence of variety was a feature of other ancient texts. Guy Deutscher has studied the grammar of documents in Hittite and Akkadian, dating back to the third millennium BC, and found in the oldest texts the same reliance on simple statements, the same absence of subordinate clauses. Some oral languages of Australian Aborigines are said to lack subordinates, and, controversially but persuasively, Daniel Everett claims the Piraha tribe don't use subordinates.[1] So the evidence points to variation of sentence structure being a relatively recent innovation in human language, one created and encouraged by writing and not the invention of writing but writing as it developed.

This flies in the face of linguists' customary bland assurance that all languages are equally complex. Not, it seems, so. Far from being fixed by innate programming, our grammatical expertise seems to have become much greater in written forms of the language over the past few thousand years, our sentences having become much more sophisticated in the way they interweave phrases and layers. It seems that writing has given human grammar a push up the evolutionary ladder.

---

1   Deutscher, *Syntactic Change in Akkadian*; Everett, *Language*, p. 287.

11 Structure

So far, this book has described the rules governing the separate word classes. This chapter looks at how everything fits together.

I have fortunately vague memories from my schooldays of being taught several different and it seemed to me equally pointless ways of trying to analyse the structure of sentences. One method was to identify the subject and the predicate – the predicate being basically everything apart from the subject, so that in the boy-and-ball example, 'the boy' is the subject and 'kicked the ball' is the predicate. Another distinction I was taught was between a phrase, which didn't have a verb in it, and a clause, which did. That was about the extent of it, or at least as far as I dimly recall.

These traditional categories and terms still exist but they have been recast by modern linguistics, which tends to take the sentence as the overall unit but sometimes accepts the clause as the main structure instead. For example, *The Cambridge Grammar of the English Language* talks in terms of clauses, which it defines, rather traditionally, as a subject plus a predicate.[1] Harking back to the good old days, another grammar defines a clause as 'a unit structured around a verb phrase'.[2] A main clause can stand alone, a subordinate clause depends on a main.

But sentences and clauses exist uninterestingly at the top of a pyramid. Modern linguistics has focussed on the components below

---

1   Rodney Huddlestone and Geoffrey K. Pullum, *The Cambridge Grammar of the English Language* (Cambridge University Press, 2002), pp. 44–45.

2   Biber et al., *Longman Grammar of Spoken and Written English*, p.120

clause/sentence level and has found that the structure of sentences – all sentences in all languages – can be formed into a hierarchy, of phrases and heads of phrases. This is a hierarchy best presented in a tree diagram.

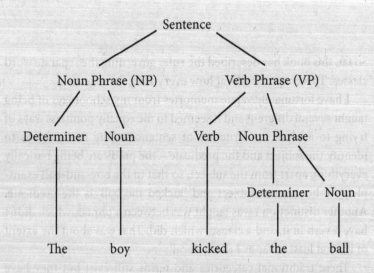

Such tree diagrams faithfully replicate the hierarchical tree structures which Herbert Simon identified as the form that evolves naturally in complex systems, because it is the simplest and quickest method of a system gaining complexity and the most stable. Hence the hierarchical tree-structuring in atoms, galaxies, biology, commercial organisations and social institutions – and language.[3]

Each phrase is based on a dominant word, called the head. A phrase is a segment of a sentence rather than a string of words; indeed, a phrase can consist of only one word. In 'He kicked it', the structure of the sentence is the same – NP + VP + NP – but now each phrase consists of a one-word head.

---

3   Herbert Simon, 'The Architecture of Complexity' (1962).

Importantly, phrases can contain other phrases, which is a fundamental instance of the principle of recursion usually considered intrinsic to language. Recursion is Chomsky's last remaining candidate as a universal property (though even that is vigorously disputed by Daniel Everett). It is also the simplest way of guaranteeing the infinite product of a grammar's finite rules, by adding potentially never-ending recursive phrases along the lines of 'the house that Jack built' or prepositional sequences like 'behind the fridge, beside the skirting board, despite the caustic soda, between the wall and the socket, to the right of the first attempt at poison, next to the cable that goes behind the . . .' ad, potentially, infinitum.

The subject–predicate distinction, first made by the grammarians of classical Greece, still forms the basis of this 'phrase-structure' analysis, though rejigged as the noun phrase and the verb phrase. There are three other types of phrase: adjectival, adverbial and prepositional.

Noun phrase	[the boy], [the small, tousle-haired, sociopathic boy], [boys]
Verb phrase	[kicked the ball], [booted it], [hoofed it blindly]
Adjectival phrase	these are usually found after the verb 'to be': he is [clumsy], he is [sorry about the window]
Adverbial phrase	[very clumsily], [unluckily], [sadly for him]
Prepositional phrase	these almost always start with the preposition: [into the window], [before he could run away]

Most grammatical analyses of modern linguistics have been based on phrase structures and, until recently, have reliably represented them in tree diagrams. There are some indications that phrase-structure analysis might be superseded, but just what by remains very unclear as I write in 2013. Perhaps by 2023 a new kind of analysis and diagram will have replaced phrase structure and its trees. But in the meantime, this is what linguistics has worked with, and very effectively, especially with Indo-European languages and especially English – small wonder given that it was developed by English-speaking linguists.

But phrase structure analysis was only the start for Noam Chomsky, who moved on in the 1960s to announce a truly grand claim: these structures, with their tree diagrams, were merely the surface representations of a 'deep structure' where the rules and constraints of our universal grammar and our innate knowledge operated. Chomsky maintained that it was this deep structure that generated the meaning of a sentence, the surface structure concerning itself with the particular operations and words of the individual language. This meant that the deep structure had to be converted into the surface structure – doing so, according to Chomsky, by a series of what he called 'transformations'. And thus was born transformational grammar, which was the method Chomsky would use in his search for the innate principles and parameters of humans' universal grammar and their application. That would be their application mainly in English, of course. Chomsky saw no pressing need to seek out exotic, non-Indo-European languages. His real interest has never been individual languages so much as the prewired principles supposedly underlying them. Moreover, the one language he has concentrated on is an idealised English, whose rules and operations are to be studied only in the abstract, never in any actual usage. Chomsky's interest was in what he called our language 'competence', not the messily inadequate, faltering business of 'performance'.

So, equipped with the various maps he has drawn up himself of the treasure island that has existed only in his own head, Chomsky has pursued his quest for the non-existent principles and features of an entirely illusory universal grammar and the ingeniously wrought transformations that would explain how these fanciful creations born of a mistaken assumption were supposed to be converted into actual – well, idealised – language.

It's no wonder Chomsky assumed that newborn infants came equipped with the almost mystical gifts of a magnificently equipped grammar module, if he thought that at some 'deep' level children were undertaking his kind of incredibly complicated information systems analysis to assemble a sentence.

Although Chomsky's transformational grammar was the orthodoxy in linguistics for a long time, it has come under increasing attack. So effectively so that, although there are old Chomskyites still publishing books and exploring what little remains of his discredited notions, during the last twenty, thirty years linguistics has moved on, under the impetus especially of cognitive linguistics, which tries to match language with neuroscience.

The new post-Chomsky, anti-Chomsky ideas have so far remained the preserve of academics who have failed to alert the public at large about what they've been up to. One reason is that their analyses are still at the forbiddingly technical stage. Another is that a new orthodoxy has yet to emerge. There are now a good dozen competing theories about grammar: systemic functional grammar, word grammar, head-driven phrase-structure grammar, the various brands of construction grammar, etc., etc.

Many of these new theories are still based on heads and phrases, and some still use phrase-structure analysis and tree diagrams, but a few have taken more radical approaches and have tried new forms of representing what they think is going on. Construction grammar, which posits that our grammar is based on core constructions rather than rules, analyses by distinctive diagrams, and adapts phrase-structure trees so that they have 'feature structures' at the nodes. Word grammar shows the dependencies between words instead of segmenting into phrases, and has a different notation with curved lines linking elements together.

One of the most interesting of the new theories is role-and-reference grammar, developed in the 1980s and 1990s by William Foley and Robert Van Valin. Whereas most linguists base their analyses on English and maybe some other Indo-European languages, Foley and Van Valin investigated grammar functions from different linguistic families from all over the world, taking them on their own terms rather than imposing Indo-European-based preconceptions.

As a basic example, all modern linguistics had assumed that the dominant component in a sentence is the subject. But in some languages, there is no such thing as the subject of a sentence. So instead of the basic unit of the noun phrase, role-and-reference grammar has the more general category, 'reference phrase', and instead of the usual distinction of subject and object, has the new categories of 'actor' and 'undergoer'. In place of phrase structure, Foley and Van Valin came up with a different, head-free model based on the concept of the core of a sentence and the periphery. Take the sentence, 'The boy kicked the ball into the window.' The core of the sentence is 'the boy kicked the ball', the periphery 'into the window'. (The periphery is conventionally analysable as a prepositional phrase like that one.) The core has a nucleus, which will usually be a verb and will contain the reference phrase(s).

Similarly, the various theories of dependency grammar take the approach that structures are based on verbs rather than the noun phrases of subjects and objects. One of these theories is word grammar, which has been developed by Richard Hudson at University College London. Like all dependency grammars, word grammar focusses on individual words and the dependent relations between words. It still accepts the idea of heads of phrases but otherwise departs from phrase-structure grammar, and has no truck with phrasal nodes. Like role and reference grammar, word grammar embraces the variety of human languages and finds that the conventional 'universal' categories don't fit very well.

The most promising of all the new theories could well be neurocognitive grammar, which looks at language from the perspective of neuroscience. Like word grammar and several other theories, this sees grammar, like all language, as a network rather than a system of rules, a network operated by our own neural networks, and one which is learned, not innate, and part of the general cognitive process, not the product of a Language Acquisition Device or any other separate language module.

This is a school that demands the imposition of first scientific principles: '(1) Start from concrete, observable phenomena; (2) Observe.'[4] In addition, any ideas about how a grammar works must first be tested for neurological plausibility. But it's not just grammar that has to be subjected to scientific, objective testing; linguistic notions themselves have to be treated with scientific rigour and all unfounded preconceptions disposed of. So neurocognitive grammar denies the validity of traditional terms like 'word' or 'meaning'. The neurocognitive school even denies that there can be such a thing as a 'language' – only the observable individual linguistic systems that operate in variously successful communication attempts with other observable individual linguistic systems.

Another basic premise is that although the brain is capable of understanding and producing symbols, actual symbols, including grammatical rules, are to be discounted, because they are abstracts, not to be found within any physical network in the brain. So where conventional linguistic analysis would concentrate on the abstract

---

4   Sydney Lamb, 'Being Realistic, Being Scientific', in *LACUS Forum 32: Networks*, ed. Shin Ja Hwang, William J. Sullivan and Arle R. Lommel (Linguistic Association of Canada and the United States, 2006), available online at www.ruf.rice.edu/~lngbrain/real.pdf

forms, categories and properties of language, neurocognitive grammar sticks to its scientific, physical remit and aspires to identify the brain systems, the connections organised in networks, that produce the networks of grammatical language.

Neuroscience and linguistics are going to have to come to depend on each other much more, otherwise both disciplines could be stalled, just as theoretical physics has been since the 1970s, when theory leapt beyond observation and experiment. Theoretical grammarians could well be fated to flounder around, tempted by one analysis after another. As neuroscience has already discovered, brain-imaging techniques are revealing with increasing accuracy where activity is happening in the brain, but they can't show what is happening. The hope is that by teaming neuroscience up with linguistics, which studies the product of that activity, the new discipline of neurolinguistics will be able to build a bridge between the two approaches and move on towards understanding the actual processes of our brains. Technical and abstruse they may well be, but neurocognitive grammar and the other new cognitive-based grammar theories are at the very forefront of scientific research into how our brains work and how they produce talking and thinking us.

Appendix 1

Some of the most common 'mistakes'
made by non-standard speakers

Here are some of the most common and conspicuous differences
between standard and non-standard English.

The non-standard column would have looked very different
even a hundred years ago, with many, many entries for each
feature. However, such has been the dramatic impact of dialect
levelling, with many of the non-standard varieties of English now
sharing the same forms, that there's almost a one-to-one corre-
spondence now between standard and effectively a standard
non-standard.

The entries in the non-standard column are linguistically
completely valid. However, most people aren't aware of that and
assume that they are mistakes, and not only mistakes but symptoms
of some sort of undesirable characteristic; of laziness, ignorance or
stupidity, or, at the least, a lack of education and intellectual as well
as social sophistication. They will be accepted perfectly happily by
non-standard, below-middle-class speakers but not in any middle-
class context and would all certainly be marked as mistakes in any
form of written English.

Non-standard	Standard
'them' with nouns	'those'
('them shoes', 'them books')	('those shoes', 'those books')

no plural with measurements ('three mile', 'five pound')	plurals ('three miles', 'five pounds')
'what' as relative pronoun ('The ball what the boy kicked')	'which'/'that' ('The ball which/that the boy kicked')
'ain't'/'in't'	'am/is/are not', 'has/have not'
'never' as a negative in the past tense ('I never talked to him')	'did not' ('I didn't talk to him')
double negatives ('I didn't see nothing')	single negatives ('I didn't see anything')
'there is/there was' with plural subjects ('There was lots of them')	'there are/there were' ('There were lots of them')
adverbs with the same form as adjectives ('I walked quick', 'he spoke slow')	adverbs adding 'ly' ('I walked quickly', 'he spoke slowly')
object pronouns in subject positions with 'and' ('Him and me are friends') (Also used by standard speakers but thought to be an error, and noticeable if delivered in a non-standard dialect)	subject pronouns in subject positions ('He and I are friends')

Non-standard speakers should bear in mind the standard version of the pronoun table (see Chapter 6), the verb 'to be' (see Chapter 7) and the past and past participle forms of the irregular verbs in standard in Appendix 2.

Appendix 2

List of irregular verbs in standard English

Basic	Simple Past Tense	Past Participle
Arise	Arose	Arisen
Awake	Awoke/awaked	Awoken/awaked
Be	Was	Been
Bear	Bore	Born
Beat	Beat	Beaten
Become	Became	Become
Begin	Began	Begun
Bend	Bent	Bent
Bet	Betted/bet	Betted/bet
Bid	Bid	Bid
Bind	Bound	Bound
Bite	Bit	Bitten
Bleed	Bled	Bled
Blow	Blew	Blown
Break	Broke	Broken
Breed	Bred	Bred
Bring	Brought	Brought
Broadcast	Broadcast	Broadcast
Browbeat	Browbeat	Browbeaten

Basic	Simple Past Tense	Past Participle
Build	Built	Built
Burn	Burned/burnt	Burned/burnt
Burst	Burst	Burst
Buy	Bought	Bought
Cast	Cast	Cast
Catch	Caught	Caught
Choose	Chose	Chosen
Cling	Clung	Clung
Come	Came	Come
Cost	Cost	Cost
Creep	Crept	Crept
Cut	Cut	Cut
Deal	Dealt	Dealt
Dig	Dug	Dug
Do	Did	Done
Draw	Drew	Drawn
Dream	Dreamed/dreamt	Dreamed/dreamt
Drink	Drank	Drunk
Drive	Drove	Driven
Dwell	Dwelled/dwelt	Dwelled/dwelt
Eat	Ate	Eaten
Fall	Fell	Fallen
Feed	Fed	Fed
Feel	Felt	Felt
Fight	Fought	Fought
Find	Found	Found
Flee	Fled	Fled
Fling	Flung	Flung
Fly	Flew	Flown
Forbear	Forbore	Forborne

LIST OF IRREGULAR VERBS IN STANDARD ENGLISH

Basic	Simple Past Tense	Past Participle
Forbid	Forbade/forbad	Forbidden
Foresee	Foresaw	Foreseen
Foretell	Foretold	Foretold
Forget	Forgot	Forgotten
Forgive	Forgave	Forgiven
Forsake	Forsook	Forsaken
Freeze	Froze	Frozen
Get	Got	Got
Gild	Gilded/gilt	Gilded/gilt
Give	Gave	Given
Go	Went	Gone
Grind	Ground	Ground
Grow	Grew	Grown
Hang	Hung	Hung
Have	Had	Had
Hear	Heard	Heard
Hew	Hewed	Hewed/hewn
Hide	Hid	Hidden
Hit	Hit	Hit
Hold	Held	Held
Hurt	Hurt	Hurt
Inset	Inset	Inset
Interweave	Interwove	Interwoven
Keep	Kept	Kept
Kneel	Knelt	Knelt
Knit	Knitted/knit	Knitted/knit
Know	Knew	Known
Lay	Laid	Laid
Lead	Led	Led
Lean	Leaned/leant	Leaned/lent
Leap	Leaped/leapt	Leaped/leapt

Basic	Simple Past Tense	Past Participle
Learn	Learned/learnt	Learned/learnt
Leave	Left	Left
Lend	Lent	Lent
Let	Let	Let
Lie	Lay	Lain
Light	Lighted/lit	Lighted/lit
Lose	Lost	Lost
Make	Made	Made
Mean	Meant	Meant
Meet	Met	Met
Miscast	Miscast	Miscast
Mishear	Misheard	Misheard
Mislay	Mislaid	Mislaid
Misread	Misread	Misread
Misspell	Misspelled/misspelt	Misspelled/misspelt
Misspend	Misspent	Misspent
Mistake	Mistook	Mistaken
Misunderstand	Misunderstood	Misunderstood
Mow	Mowed	Mowed/mown
Outdo	Outdid	Outdone
Outgrow	Outgrew	Outgrown
Outrun	Outran	Outrun
Outsell	Outsold	Outsold
Outshine	Outshone	Outshone
Overbid	Overbid	Overbid
Overcome	Overcame	Overcome
Overdo	Overdid	Overdone
Overdraw	Overdrew	Overdrawn
Overeat	Overate	Overeaten
Overfly	Overflew	Overflown

LIST OF IRREGULAR VERBS IN STANDARD ENGLISH

Basic	Simple Past Tense	Past Participle
Overhang	Overhung	Overhung
Overhear	Overheard	Overheard
Overlay	Overlaid	Overlaid
Overlie	Overlay	Overlain
Overpay	Overpaid	Overpaid
Override	Overrode	Overridden
Overrun	Overran	Overrun
Overshoot	Overshot	Overshot
Overtake	Overtook	Overtaken
Overthrow	Overthrew	Overthrown
Pay	Paid	Paid
Prove	Proved	Proved/proven
Put	Put	Put
Quit	Quitted/quit	Quitted/quit
Read	Read	Read
Rebuild	Rebuilt	Rebuilt
Recast	Recast	Recast
Redo	Redid	Redone
Rehear	Reheard	Reheard
Remake	Remade	Remade
Rend	Rent	Rent
Repay	Repaid	Repaid
Reread	Reread	Reread
Rerun	Reran	Rerun
Resell	Resold	Resold
Reset	Reset	Reset
Resit	Resat	Resat
Retake	Retook	Retaken
Retell	Retold	Retold
Rewrite	Rewrote	Rewritten

Basic	Simple Past Tense	Past Participle
Rid	Rid	Rid
Ride	Rode	Ridden
Ring	Rang	Rung
Rise	Rose	Risen
Run	Ran	Run
Saw	Sawed	Sawed/sawn
Say	Said	Said
Seek	Sought	Sought
Sell	Sold	Sold
Send	Sent	Sent
Set	Set	Set
Sew	Sewed	Sewed/sewn
Shake	Shook	Shaken
Shear	Sheared	Sheared/shorn
Shed	Shed	Shed
Shine	Shone	Shone
Shit	Shat	Shat
Shoe	Shoed/shod	Shoed/shod
Shoot	Shot	Shot
Show	Showed	Showed/shown
Shrink	Shrank	Shrunk
Shut	Shut	Shut
Sing	Sang	Sung
Sink	Sank	Sunk
Sit	Sat	Sat
Sleep	Slept	Slept
Slide	Slid	Slid
Slink	Slunk	Slunk
Slit	Slit	Slit
Smell	Smelled/smelt	Smelled/smelt

LIST OF IRREGULAR VERBS IN STANDARD ENGLISH

Basic	Simple Past Tense	Past Participle
Smite	Smote	Smitten
Sow	Sowed	Sowed/sown
Speak	Spoke	Spoken
Speed	Speeded/sped	Speeded/sped
Spell	Spelled/spelt	Spelled/spelt
Spend	Spent	Spent
Spill	Spilled/spilt	Spilled/spilt
Spin	Spun	Spun
Spit	Spat	Spat
Split	Split	Split
Spoil	Spoiled/spoilt	Spoiled/spoilt
Spread	Spread	Spread
Spring	Sprang	Sprung
Stand	Stood	Stood
Steal	Stole	Stolen
Stick	Stuck	Stuck
Sting	Stung	Stung
Stink	Stank/stunk	Stunk
Strew	Strewed	Strewed/strewn
Stride	Strode	Stridden
Strike	Struck	Struck
String	Strung	Strung
Strive	Strove	Striven
Sublet	Sublet	Sublet
Swear	Swore	Sworn
Sweep	Swept	Swept
Swell	Swelled	Swelled/swollen
Swim	Swam	Swum
Swing	Swung	Swung
Take	Took	Taken

Basic	Simple Past Tense	Past Participle
Teach	Taught	Taught
Tear	Tore	Torn
Tell	Told	Told
Think	Thought	Thought
Throw	Threw	Thrown
Thrust	Thrust	Thrust
Tread	Trod	Trodden/trod
Underbid	Underbid	Underbid
Undercut	Undercut	Undercut
Undergo	Underwent	Undergone
Underlie	Underlay	Underlain
Underpay	Underpaid	Underpaid
Undersell	Undersold	Undersold
Understand	Understood	Understood
Undertake	Undertook	Undertaken
Underwrite	Underwrote	Underwritten
Undo	Undid	Undone
Unstick	Unstuck	Unstuck
Unwind	Unwound	Unwound
Uphold	Upheld	Upheld
Upset	Upset	Upset
Wake	Waked/woke	Waked/woken
Waylay	Waylaid	Waylaid
Wear	Wore	Worn
Weave	Weaved/wove	Weaved/woven
Wed	Wedded/wed	Wedded/wed
Weep	Wept	Wept
Wet	Wetted/wet	Wetted/wet
Win	Won	Won
Wind	Wound	Wound

LIST OF IRREGULAR VERBS IN STANDARD ENGLISH

Basic	Simple Past Tense	Past Participle
Withdraw	Withdrew	Withdrawn
Withhold	Withheld	Withheld
Withstand	Withstood	Withstood
Wring	Wrung	Wrung
Write	Wrote	Written

Rare and/or recently regularised

Abide	Abode	Abode
Befall	Befell	Befallen
Beget	Begot	Begotten
Behold	Beheld	Beheld
Beseech	Besought	Besought
Beset	Beset	Beset
Bespeak	Bespoke	Bespoken
Bid	Bade	Bidden
Chide	Chid	Chidden
Cleave	Clove/cleft	Cloven/cleft
Slay	Slew	Slain

Acknowledgements

My thanks to my agent, David Miller, to Becky Walsh, Caro Westmore and Rosie Gailer at John Murray and especially to my editor, Roland Philipps. Thanks also to the ever-helpful staff at the British Library.

Ali G's interview with Heinz Wolff from Channel 4's 11 O'Clock Show reprinted courtesy of Talkback, part of Fremantle Media Limited.

Finally, my heartfelt gratitude to Tracey, David and Alec for all their help.